T0345530

PARACELSUS

☞ Books in the RENAISSANCE LIVES series explore and illustrate the life histories and achievements of significant artists, intellectuals and scientists in the early modern world. They delve into literature, philosophy, the history of art, science and natural history and cover narratives of exploration, statecraft and technology.

Series Editor: François Quiviger

Already published

Blaise Pascal: Miracles and Reason *Mary Ann Caws*

Caravaggio and the Creation of Modernity *Troy Thomas*

Donatello and the Dawn of Renaissance Art *A. Victor Coonin*

Hieronymus Bosch: Visions and Nightmares *Nils Büttner*

Isaac Newton and Natural Philosophy *Niccolò Guicciardini*

John Evelyn: A Life of Domesticity *John Dixon Hunt*

Leonardo da Vinci: Self, Art and Nature *François Quiviger*

Michelangelo and the Viewer in His Time *Bernadine Barnes*

Paracelsus: An Alchemical Life *Bruce T. Moran*

Petrarch: Everywhere a Wanderer *Christopher S. Celenza*

Pieter Bruegel and the Idea of Human Nature *Elizabeth Alice Honig*

Raphael and the Antique *Claudia La Malfa*

Rembrandt's Holland *Larry Silver*

Titian's Touch: Art, Magic and Philosophy *Maria L. Loh*

PARACELSUS

An Alchemical Life

BRUCE T. MORAN

REAKTION BOOKS

For Ben and Bertie, who love to wander and explore

Published by Reaktion Books Ltd
Unit 32, Waterside
44–48 Wharf Road
London N1 7UX, UK
www.reaktionbooks.co.uk

First published 2019

Printed and bound in China

A catalogue record for this book is available from the British Library

ISBN 978 1 78914 144 3

COVER: Anonymous, undated portrait of Paracelsus (after a 16th-century engraving), oil on wood. Private collection (photo Heritage Images/Fine Art Images/akg-images).

CONTENTS

ALTERIVS NON SIT, QVI SVVS ESSE POTEST.

OMNE DONVM PERFECTVM Á DEO, IMPERF. Á DIABO.

AVREOLVS PHILIPPVS THEOPHRASTVS

LAVS DEO, PAX VIVIS, REQVIES ÆTERNA SEPVLTIS.

ZOTH

Introduction: Bones

ones! Just bones. Whoever ransacked Salzburg's prominent castle, the Hohensalzburg Fortress, in the days following the American occupation of the city at the end of the Second World War must have been very disappointed, if not dismayed. It was, after all, treasure, not bones, that he was looking for. The location looked promising and pointed to a real prize. The intruder found a small door in a room, the castle's room number thirteen, where precious objects had been kept, and behind it, set down in a shaft, rested a wooden crate. The crate, filled with shavings, contained a metal box. Surely this was it, something worth a fortune. But then, bones! Just bones.

In Salzburg in 1945, bones in a box did not make great plunder, so the pillager tossed them aside. When this was noticed soon thereafter, the castle's curator knew what he had to do to keep the bones out of the wrong hands. According to one account, he buried them, this time under a pile of rubble in the castle's basement. In another, he took them home to his apartment and hid them. Maybe he did both. When things were safer, they could once again come to light. These were, after all, not just any bones, but bones that had once belonged to one of the most extraordinary characters of the European

1 Woodcut portrait of Paracelsus by an anonymous artist, *c.* 1567.

Renaissance, a physician, alchemist and religious philosopher named Theophrastus von Hohenheim (1493–1541), who later became known as Paracelsus (a Latinized reference to his German name – literally high, or perhaps alpine home – or, as some others would allege, a claim to being above or beyond Celsus, the first-century AD Roman physician).

Paracelsus had died in Salzburg in September 1541, several days after dictating his last will and testament while sitting on a traveller's cot at an inn called The White Rose. He wanted to be buried in the cemetery of a local church, St Sebastian. The bones have been at St Sebastian, with brief intermissions, ever since. At first they rested outside the church and then, in the mid-eighteenth century, when the church was rebuilt and enlarged, were transferred to a new monument, a marble pyramid in the church's vestibule. The monument had a little door, and Paracelsus' box of bones could be, with proper permission, easily removed. Generations of scholars have been unable to keep their hands off them. An examination in the nineteenth century suggested a suspicious death, indeed murder. More recent examinations have suggested that Paracelsus may have been intersex: the pelvis appeared characteristically female.[1] Whatever the truth of the latter claim, the first is certainly false. Damage to the skull, considered by some to have been the result of a blow to the head, occurred, we now know, after his body's interment. The real cause of his death remains uncertain, but a toxic level (ten times the normal amount) of mercury found in his bones, the result of long exposure, suggests a contributing factor.

Paracelsus left behind not just bones but texts, and like the examination of physical remains, the analysis of his written remains has led to widely varying interpretations. Each new inquiry locates Paracelsus in a different place. That is because the real Paracelsus does not want us to find him. In relation to his own world, he was forever 'alone and foreign and different'.[2] As one Paracelsus scholar notes, 'Everyone knows something to say about him, and yet no one really knows him. We get close to him with difficulty, but, having met him, we just can't get away from him.'[3] What we don't know, we sometimes invent. He becomes a lonely genius whose ideas are far ahead of their time; a Romantic hero defying convention and established authority; a Renaissance magician; a martyr of natural science; a religious militant; a Utopian rebel and an advocate for social change. As a physician, he gets imagined as a precursor of modern medicine, one of the many 'fathers' of enlightened medical practice, or as a forerunner of holistic approaches to healing. He is transformed in portraits, literature and film and at one point gets turned into an icon of mass ideology, refashioned, during the Nazi era, as a German national idol. No wonder, then, that shortly before the bombs started falling on Salzburg, his bones were once again removed from their pyramid tomb and carried up the hill for safekeeping in room number thirteen of the Salzburg castle.

In Paracelsus, we meet mystery, magic, craft and profound insight. But we can only really know him on his own terms. The modern world has become too precise in defining what belongs to medicine and science to help much in overcoming the perceived paradox of Paracelsus: namely, that one of the most important figures during the Renaissance to argue for changes in the way the body was understood, nature studied, disease defined and new therapies devised was himself moved by mystical speculations, an alchemical view of nature and a view of creation that required human beings to complete what a divine creator had begun. We have to take off our twenty-first-century spectacles to keep him in sight. Only then does the worth and relevance of what he did come into view, and only then can we recognize how an amalgam of characteristics made him appear so eccentric and dangerous to his contemporaries.

Part of what makes Paracelsus unique is his embrace of what, to many, appeared to be opposites. He combined practices that were magical and empirical, scholarly and folk, learned and artisanal. He knew Latin (the language of scholars) but wrote and lectured in German. He read ancient medical texts and then burned 'the best of them' in a public display of reproach. The most important text for any physician, he argued, was not one found in a library. Although raised in the Catholic faith, he was anti-papal, shared many views in common with Reformation theologians and believed devoutly in a female deity, picturing Mary as a the pre-existing spouse of God the Father within the Sacred Trinity. In addition, he challenged the habits of conventional learning and educated behaviour. He admired the know-how and insights of those who worked with their hands – such as miners, bathers, alchemists, midwives and barber surgeons – and he taught his students to learn the medical art not on the basis of an ancient medical canon, but from experience. He travelled constantly, was hardly ever in one place for long, and had a reputation for lingering in taverns and drinking to excess. He often wrote by means of dictation, and most of his books went unpublished during his lifetime. Magical, religious and scientific traditions merged in those writings, as did the subjects of alchemy, astronomy, philosophy and medicine. Those combinations produced theoretical reforms – in regard to understanding the operations of the body, making medicines and curing illness – that clashed with the theory and practice of traditional learning. He therefore made enemies, and the attacks of his rivals were pitiless: he was, according to them, no more than a peasant; he was not even a man since, they said, he had lost his testicles while herding geese as a boy; he dictated while in a drunken stupor in the middle of the night while thrashing about with his sword; and he made pacts with the Devil and practised the black arts. In defending himself Paracelsus gave as good as he got, mocking the ignorance of his accusers with a language that was rough, irreverent and often foul. He was not, he admitted, raised in silk garments, but had grown up wearing coarse cloth.

He was born in the little Swiss town of Einsiedeln, and if you travel there today, you may drive along the shore of Lake Zurich and be stunned into silence by a landscape awesome in a beauty that merges earth and sky. Paracelsus experienced this. He drew life from it, and the union of heaven and earth stands out as a significant part of his conception of nature and the body. Each person, he argued, was a microcosm, a condensation of the entire universe. It is easy to get that feeling as the mountains knit together the terrestrial and celestial realms around Einsiedeln.

Paracelsus' father, Wilhelm, was an illegitimate son of a noble family (the Bombasts) that resided at Hohenheim, a town near Stuttgart in an area of Germany proud of its ancient culture and dialect. His mother, meanwhile, was Swiss and a bond servant at the local cloister. What brought the two together will probably never be known. It was the custom of the day, however, that the child of a marriage like this one, in which the parents came from unequal social ranks, was considered automatically to belong to the lower social order. Paracelsus, in other words, had the status of a bond servant, a semi-serf, and legally belonged to a feudal lord. This is why, on Paracelsus' death, the legal representative of the Abbot of Einsiedeln had every right, by ancient feudal custom, to claim the best material item that his bond servant still possessed at death. He acquired a silver cup that weighed five and a half loth. It also may help explain something else. Several portraits of Paracelsus made during his lifetime bear an inscription that conveys rich meaning, given his social circumstances, and that may have become something like a personal motto: *Alterius non sit qui suus esse potest* ('Let him not be another's who can be his own'; or, more loosely but better suited to the feudal identity of his birth, 'Let him not belong to another who is able to possess himself') (illus. 2).

Wilhelm practised medicine in Einsiedeln and called his son Theophrastus, possibly a reminder of the ancient medical botanist by the same name. The other names, Philippus and Aureolus, that later shaped his unique persona as Philippus Aureolus Theophrastus Bombastus von Hohenheim may or may not have been there all along. His mother died when he was about ten years old. Soon thereafter, he and his father moved to the Austrian province of Carinthia and to a town called Villach. His father remained there practising medicine for 32 years, and there he died in September 1534. Along the way, Paracelsus learnt Latin in school and possibly much else from learned clerics within range. However, most of what he knew about nature and the body in these early years he learnt from his father. By the time he was sixteen, he was ready for university and, according to his own account, began studies at the Italian university of Ferrara, earning a medical degree there as a doctor of both traditional medicine and surgery. That, at least, is what he tells us, but no records at Ferrara have yet been found that support the claim. Separating fact from fiction is a challenge when reconstructing Paracelsus' biography, and some depictions have been too quick to repeat what should properly fall into the category of legend. When tempted to trust the self-portrait that Paracelsus provides, it is best always to be on one's guard. After all, part of the project of possessing himself required constructing a personal history and credible identity that could give weight to the ideas he advanced. Simply put, Paracelsus sometimes made himself up. What is not disputed, however, is that his life very soon became one of near-constant wandering as he studied the book of Nature by observing and learning from those who had experience of nature's secrets, but who seldom wrote books of their own.

From time to time, he came to rest, and in 1538, tired and nearing the end of a controversial and turbulent life, Paracelsus was back in Carinthia, a region he regarded as his second home, if he ever had a home. He spent some time once again in Villach and in another small town named St Veit, and from there, weary of the reprimands and scoldings of university physicians who had come to despise him, he announced plans to publish several treatises at once, in one big book. One of the included texts aimed at exposing the medical errors of his detractors.

2 Likeness of Paracelsus by the monogrammist AH, dated 1538.

In another, *Septem defensiones* (Seven Defences), he sought to defend his own thoughts and actions against those who had long sought to discredit them. To get his collection published, he turned to the 'archbishops, bishops, prelates, dukes, barons, lords, and knights of the archduchy', explaining that his enemies had prevented the publication of his volume anywhere in the German nation.[4] The Carinthian nobility and social elite agreed to help and promised to supply funds in order to get the book into print. But time slipped by, and by the end of 1541 Paracelsus was dead. The project was forgotten – or, we might more charitably say, delayed – until 1955, when the modern state of Carinthia made good on the promise that had been made 417 years earlier by publishing a special edition of the book called *Die Kärntner Schriften* (The Carinthian Writings). By the mid-twentieth century, of course, Paracelsus had, bones aside, turned to dust, and in 1541, as he was laid to rest in St Sebastian church, the *Seven Defences* amounted only to a pile of handwritten papers left behind to gather the same.

But not for long. Soon the hunt would be on for Paracelsus' writings of all sorts, and in 1564 a physician named Theodor Byrckmann, whose father, conveniently, ran a printing house in Cologne, discovered this pile of papers, knocked off the dust and published the text. The *Seven Defences* has been reprinted numerous times since, and I have chosen to use it here as a means to reconstruct the debates and controversies that touched upon Paracelsus' intellectual, moral and emotional life, and that are essential for understanding what was at stake in the reception of his ideas. This treatise thus becomes for us seven windows through which we gain glimpses of specific ideas, practices and associations that were both exciting and threatening to the world in which Paracelsus lived. What we see through each may seem strange, since this is a world of witches, magic, occult powers, alchemy and natural spirits. Nevertheless, through each, we also get a clear view of a broader landscape made up of the three most profoundly transformative movements of the late Renaissance: scientific revolution, religious reformation, and social and economic change. Paracelsus is involved in them all and has something to say that is relevant to each. Sometimes we may not like what we see, not least because sometimes what we witness is nothing other than the ugly street life of competing ideas and spoiled aspirations, the furious altercations that arouse insults and injuries. Paracelsus is often angry. As we will see, he has a lot to be upset about.

The following chapters present a broad outline of the life and ideas of Theophrastus von Hohenheim, called Paracelsus. This book is intended for those who may know something or nothing at all about him. Thus, before engaging with the specific issues and disputes that make up his respective quarrels and defences, we will need to get our feet on the ground by learning something about the context (the medical, social, religious, political and scientific backgrounds) in which many of those controversies took place and that made them both renowned and notorious. Most of the chapters will begin with a general description of a particular aspect of the Renaissance world into which Paracelsus was born. It will then focus on how Paracelsus attempted to change it. Having seen what Paracelsus set out to do to the world around him will allow us, in the final chapter, to take note of what the world, following his death, has done to him. The tools of art, literature, theatre, film and, of course, the often passionate sentiments involved in historical writing have invented and reinvented Paracelsus. This is the Paracelsus that enters popular culture, the Paracelsus that continues to fascinate and have meaning within worlds far removed from anything he would ever have known.

ONE

Medicine Lost in a Labyrinth and the Defence of Defiant Healing

Theophrastus von Hohenheim, later called Paracelsus, was probably less than 1.5 metres tall (5 feet), and by comparison, the sword he carried must have seemed enormous. Rumour had it that he kept a medicine in the sword's pommel capable of curing almost anything. Why not? The Renaissance world was one of wonders and marvels, a world in which the old and trusted mixed with the new and unexpected. Theophrastus drew breath from this world and flourished in its discoveries and delights. He was born at the very end of 1493, although the precise date is uncertain, at a time when the Italian mathematician Luca Pacioli (1447–1517) was standardizing the accounting technique of double-entry bookkeeping that fuelled a new market economy. Pacioli's friend Leonardo da Vinci (1452–1519) was designing a colossal equestrian statue for the Sforza Duke of Milan, imagining machines of war and industry and dreaming of making it possible for people to fly. Further south, Michelangelo (1475–1564) had just bought a large block of marble with the intention of carving an imposing statue of Hercules and was, along with Leonardo and many others, representing the world in three dimensions by means of the method of perspective drawing. In 1493 Christopher Columbus (1451–1506) had only recently arrived back in Spain and was composing a letter concerning his observations of the island he called 'Hispana' (now known as Hispaniola, the island shared by the Dominican Republic and Haiti), noting how easy it would be to conquer the people living there. To the north, the son born earlier to Hans Luder (or Luther) and his wife, Margarethe, had just turned ten and was studying Latin. Having learnt to read and write, Martin Luther (1483–1546) would, when Paracelsus was still a young adult, occasion wrenching reforms in Christian practices and beliefs, helping to set in motion the Protestant Reformation. Times were changing, and the discoveries, inventions and new ideas that percolated throughout the world of Paracelsus were themselves all impacted by what some see as the biggest change of all: namely, a change in the organization and communication of knowledge itself, a transformation that shifted the world of learning from a culture of scribes to a culture of print.

The technology of printing with moveable type altered access to learning, ordered and organized what was read, stockpiled information and expanded the opportunities for critical discussion among an increasingly literate public. Books changed habits of education, stimulated expression and, for those willing to invest in their production, created new opportunities for making money. When Paracelsus came into the world, the number of presses in western Europe (many of the most important were in Italy, Germany and France) had grown from a single press in the German city of Mainz to around a thousand, and in the space of about fifty years these had already churned out millions of books.[1] Some of the publications were prepared by a group of scholars known as Humanists, who made it their business to rediscover and edit the works of ancient writers, believing that the oldest books were still the best and conveyed truths connected to a divinely inspired and uncorrupted wisdom. Other books excited attention by publishing reports of curiosities linked to recently discovered places and peoples. Some used pictures, woodblock engravings, to visualize what many had never seen before. Still others conveyed ideas that broke with long-accepted opinion. In 1541, the year that Paracelsus died, one such book, written by the mathematician Georg Joachim Rheticus (1514–1574), summarized ideas that were just getting formally worked out by his teacher, the Polish German astronomer and church administrator Nicholas Copernicus (1473–1543). Copernicus' own text, *De revolutionibus orbium coelestium* (On the Revolutions of the Celestial Spheres), appeared two years later, in 1543, the same year as the publication of one of the most important books in the history of anatomy, *De humani corporis fabrica* (On the Fabric of the Human Body), written by a 29-year-old Brussels-born physician teaching at the University of Padua whose name was Andries van Wesel. In Latin, he called himself Vesalius (1514–1564).

If you were curious about the world, well educated and loved learning, there was lots to be excited about, lots to enjoy, and lots to look forward to, unless, of course, you became sick. In fact, if your life was anything like that of a sixteenth-century German chronicler named Hermann von Weinsberg, you probably had not been feeling entirely well for a very long time. Remembering his childhood, Weinsberg recounted bouts with measles, dysentery, boils, nosebleeds, lesions in his mouth and gums, and infestations of lice and worms. In addition, a childhood 'pox' left him alive but killed two of his sisters. He got a hernia as a boy and it was never fixed; and then there were accidents: his head was gashed; he almost drowned; and an errant musket ball at one point grazed his cheek and skull.[2]

You might have been luckier than Weinsberg, but you could not live long without having ailments of your own. To confront them, you, like Paracelsus, might have tried local remedies or turned to a number of vernacular books offering self-help. On reaching further into the medical marketplace, you would have found bathers and barbers; those who cut for kidney and bladder stones; those who, by scraping the lens of the eye with a needle, 'couched' for cataracts; those who pulled teeth; and, of course, those who set bones, treated wounds and lesions, and occasionally amputated limbs. If you needed to see a university-trained physician, you could expect a diagnosis following the same theories that had guided medical instruction for almost two millennia; and you would probably have noticed that they advised very much the same procedures to treat your illness as to prevent it – in Paracelsus' time, prophylaxis (the techniques and regimens of preventing disease) and therapy (the means of treating disease when it occurred) were often the same thing. To figure out what was wrong, your physician would note your symptoms in terms of combinations of hot, cold, wet and dry. He (for universities at the time did not allow women) might look at your urine or faeces; observe the taste, foaminess or greasiness of your blood; feel your pulse or thump your abdomen or chest, all in an attempt to determine which 'humours' – the fluids in the body (some thought they were all in the blood) that accounted for health and illness – were out of a natural balance specific to you.

Humours were Western medicine's guiding star, and much of the conversation you had with your doctor would have been about them. The theory was ancient, developed in the fifth and fourth centuries BC by a number of writers connected to the school of the Greek physician Hippocrates (460–370 BC) and expanded upon centuries later by arguably the greatest of the ancient Greek physicians, Galen of Pergamum (AD 130–210).

According to informed humoral opinion, each person had his or her own peculiar humoral balance, but that balance could be undone by all sorts of things – diet, lifestyle, age, even the weather. So a Renaissance physician who followed Galen looked upon illness as a general disorder of humours in the body and sought ways to restore a natural balance by means of identifying which humour was out of equilibrium. Since each of the humours (usually identified as phlegm, blood, yellow bile and black bile) exhibited combinations of 'qualities' (hot, cold, wet and dry), the doctor gauged the presence of those qualities in combination (hot–dry; dry–cold; cold–wet; wet–hot) to identify the offending humour. Then, in order to deal with the problem, he would impose qualities of the opposite sort. If you presented with symptoms of cold and wet (indicative of too much phlegm), hot and dry remedies were in store for you – perhaps a change of diet with an emphasis upon hot and dry foods, maybe medicines made from plants that grew in hot and arid locations, or perhaps by bleeding from the part of the body linked to the place of that humoral excess.

Doctors loved to prescribe venesection – that is, bleeding. Different veins were believed to be connected to different organs, so that drawing blood away from them would also pull away associated humours. For liver problems, the vein in the right hand needed to be cut; for the spleen, the vein in the left. When veins were clogged by heavy humours, venesection was not enough, and Galenic doctors would order a variety of other procedures, such as scarification, cupping, blistering, purging, vomiting or sweating, to deal with the problems they caused. A trademark of Galenic practice was the letting of large amounts of blood, with decisions about how much to let depending on a variety of factors including the season, the climate, and the patient's age and gender. Some days were better for bleeding than others. In Jewish communities, Sundays, Wednesdays and Fridays were best; Christians preferred specific saints' days. Most people who could afford it were bled on a routine basis; forgetting to do so was asking for trouble. Letters between a young German man who had left home for university in the 1570s and his concerned mother show us just how much bleeding mattered: along with the usual chit-chat about laundry, clothing and things needed from home, in several of her letters, his mother included instructions about healthy living, insisting that her son be regularly bled and that he 'go bathe every month when it suits you best'. Writing home, her son promised to keep his appointment for bleeding but asked to be sent a special bloodletting lancet, particularly since, he argued, 'the other students have their own'.[3]

Paying attention to humours had guided learned medicine for centuries, and some of the ancient Hippocratic writings joined the texts of Galen and the Islamic medical authority Ibn Sīnā (also known as Avicenna, *c.* 980–1037) as standard texts of European medical education throughout the Renaissance. Major centres of medical education had long existed in places such as Montpellier, Salerno, Bologna and Padua, and since the early fourteenth century, the reading of ancient texts had been combined, in some places, with medical dissection. There was nothing new in this regard, as ancient medical learning had been largely based upon dissection (both animal and human). Indeed, two physicians working long before Galen in the city of Alexandria, Erasistratos and Herophilos, were remembered as having dissected living human subjects. Galen never went that far, but warned his students not to depend solely upon books, and rather to practise dissection, advising them to hone their skills on animals so that, when a human body became available, they were well prepared.

That message, however, got lost, at least until an Italian physician named Mondino dei Luzzi (1275–1326) reintroduced dissection as part of medical education at the University of Bologna and composed one of the first texts, called the *Anathomia*, in the history of Western medicine to be focused upon anatomy. Mondino performed the dissections himself, and his method was to dissect in sequence what he called the three 'venters' (cavities) of the body: the abdomen, thorax and cranium (areas of vital organs usually avoided by surgeons, who most often busied themselves with the body's extremities). Bologna led the way, but other universities followed suit. At Padua, dissections were a winter event, and each year the university made a male and a female cadaver available. Twenty students were allowed to observe the male dissection, thirty the female. Some anatomists at Padua and elsewhere became famous, among them Jacopo Berengario da Carpi (1460–1530); Vesalius, of course; and the Paris professor Charles Estienne (1504–1564). These physicians were active before and during Paracelsus' lifetime, and he probably knew of them and some of their books. But he would have been especially aware of one book, often used as an introductory text in medical education, that was first published in 1491. This was a collection of medical writings called *Fasciculus medicinae* (A Little Bundle of Medicine), which, in later editions, included versions of Mondino's *Anathomia*.

The *Fasciculus* was frequently republished, and when reprinted in 1493, just as Paracelsus was coming into the world, it appeared with an interesting illustration that added to its attraction and which tells us a lot about the relation between theory and practice in the medical environment that Paracelsus would later attempt to transform (illus. 3). The picture represents an anatomy lecture in which the professor of medicine speaks from a lectern, explaining the text of a medical authority. But as prominent as he is, the professor in the scene is altogether removed from the actual dissection itself – that work is being carried out by two assistants in the foreground. One assistant, sometimes called a *demonstator* and sometimes an *ostensor*, points to the actual part of the body under discussion. The other, called a *sector* or *prosector*, usually a barber or surgeon, performs the cutting.

Surgeons in Paracelsus' day were usually not trained at universities but by apprenticeship. They offered a variety of services including bandaging, bleeding, burning skin tumours and haemorrhoids, and cautery to deal with abscesses and to stop arterial haemorrhage. And, of course, they were useful on the battlefield; with the introduction of gunpowder into warfare during the Renaissance, they were especially busy. Surgeons may have been literate, but not necessarily so: they were craftsmen, not scholars. In the *Fasciculus* image, the professor reads in Latin, the scholarly language of the day and one that the *sector* most likely does not understand. The professor occupies himself with books, the *sector* with the work of the hand. Over Paracelsus' lifetime, these two realms of medical labour, the work of the mind and the work of the hand, so separate in the image, came slowly together. Paracelsus helped that happen, arguing that they should never be apart and that it is impossible to be a good physician if they are. 'Where the doctor is not also a surgeon,' he declared, 'he is an idol that is nothing but a painted monkey.'[4] Others claimed the same, less stridently perhaps, and representing medical views different from those that Paracelsus defined. By the time Vesalius published his monumental anatomical text in 1543, there was no distance remaining between the practices of mind and hand. In the image accompanying Vesalius' book, the work that had previously been left to artisan craftsmen is now being done by Vesalius himself. Look carefully and you will see one of Vesalius' hands in the abdomen of a dissected female body and his other hand pointed upwards, towards heaven. The body, a heavenly creation, is a powerful and revealing text, one just as important as any book, and one that can only be read by means of manual experience. The two former assistants, the *sector* and *demonstrator*, are now reduced to sharpening knives under the dissecting table (illus. 4).

3 Anatomical lecture, from Joannes de Ketham, *Fasciculus medicine* (1495).

4 A depiction of dissection, from Andreas Vesalius, *De humani corporis fabrica* (1543).

The first of Paracelsus' seven defences is a response to critics who had condemned him for introducing and teaching a new kind of medicine that defied ancient authority in regard to ideas about the functioning of the body and the origin and treatment of disease. The viciousness of the attacks suggests that he had achieved sufficient prominence to be regarded as a real threat to those who had medical status to lose. But where did his medical reputation come from, and what were the circumstances that gave rise to such vehement censure and denunciation?

After a period of wandering across Europe and beyond – some episodes the stuff of legend, such as his allegedly having been taken captive by Tartars on a visit to Moscow – Paracelsus arrived in Strasbourg in 1526. He acquired rights of citizenship and may have briefly established a medical practice. Certainly he took patients and treated them on the basis of techniques linked both to traditional medicine and to those he had encountered during his journeys, to the learning and procedures of military surgeons, barbers, bathers, village women, alchemists, monks and those regarded as magicians. Some of his patients exalted in his cures, especially since his procedures often avoided the uncomfortable regimes of vomiting, expulsion and bleeding prescribed by traditional doctors. His good reputation grew further as a result of a successful intervention in the case of a well-known publisher in Basel, Johann Froben (1460–1527), and a subsequent consultation with one of the most famous scholars of the time, Erasmus of Rotterdam (1466–1536). The prestige won through such interventions led, in 1527, to Paracelsus' appointment as city physician in Basel, a job that came with an invitation to become a professor of medicine at the university there. It is here that earlier currents of criticism regarding his views of the body and medical practices met a whirlpool of disapproval and conflicting sentiments. After all, the university was a bastion of Galenic medicine, and, without consulting the medical faculty, the good city fathers of Basel had invited the fox into the chicken coop.

The feathers now really began to fly, and it is easy enough to see what so alarmed the medical status quo. Advertising himself to potential students, Paracelsus proclaimed that few doctors practised medicine successfully and that most had done great harm to those who were ill. The reason for such malpractice, he argued, was that doctors had slavishly latched on to the words of Hippocrates, Galen, Avicenna and others, regarding each as some sort of oracle, and had not been willing to deviate from them by a finger's breadth. One could get a doctor's title in this way, but never become a true physician. Being a good physician was not a matter of knowing ancient languages or of comprehending the lessons of a bunch of books. What mattered was a deep understanding of nature and how it worked; only then could one know the real causes of illness and how to make truly effective medicines. To his students, Paracelsus would teach internal medicine as well as surgery, and not by way of teaching about humours or by consulting the textbooks of Hippocrates and Galen. Experience, experiment and reasoning would replace those authorities. Make your way to Basel, he announced, if you want to learn true medicine (illus. 5).[5]

The message was clear: don't study medicine with regular professors, for they know nothing; come to me instead and learn a new way, unknown to Galen and the rest, for understanding the body and treating its diseases. Paracelsus was serious about his intentions, and his colleagues (and their students) felt seriously threatened – he did not have to wait long to find out how they would react. One Sunday morning, soon after his appointment in Basel, there suddenly appeared posted on several doors around town, including the door of the Church of St Martin and St Peter, a poetic lampoon directed at the new professor of medicine. The little poem introduced the ghost of Galen writing against 'Theophrastus, or better Cacophrastus' (*caco* can mean 'bad' or 'evil', but it is probably intended here to mean 'shit'). 'Who can endure what Cacophrastus has said about my art', asks Galen's spirit. 'I did not know about peasant herbs, but I did know about hellebore [a cure for madness] which I send to you to use for your sick head.' The learning of Cacophrastus was 'peasant wisdom', and Cacophrastus himself was not worthy 'to carry the chamber pot to Hippocrates' or to herd Galen's pigs. He was a good-for-nothing, and the best thing for him would be 'a rope with which you could hang yourself, after one has recognized all your humbug.'[6]

He did not even get a lecture hall. The city might have made him a colleague, but the medical college did not have to give him a room to teach in. When students signed up for his class, he taught them off-site. There he explained a bit of Hippocrates and then moved on to other parts of medicine, including surgery. When discussing this and other subjects, he did something even more unforgiveable: he lectured not in Latin, the language of scholars, but in German, the language of barber surgeons and craftsmen. As we will see, he wrote

BASILEA

5 Basel, from Hartmann Schedel, *Liber chronicarum* (Nuremberg Chronicle, 1493).

books in German as well, just at the time when German was becoming a written language; in his own way, he helped it become one.

His teaching career at Basel was brief, limited to the summer and winter terms of 1527 and 1528. On 24 June 1527, St John's Day, he dramatized in yet another way his distaste for conventional medicine. Students were on the loose, celebrating midsummer and looking for ways to turn the world upside down. Of course, there was a bonfire for casting out evil spirits, and it must have been a carnivalesque scene as students symbolically burned things, or images of things, they did not like. Paracelsus decided that this would be a good time to make a statement to underscore his disgust of the old medical regime. In a pyrotechnic spectacle, he saw to it that what he called 'the best of books' of traditional medicine would be consumed by the flames and turned to ashes. Exactly what book went up in smoke is a subject of ongoing debate. A likely candidate, however, is an edition (perhaps a student summary) of the encyclopaedic *Canon of Medicine*, a core text of medical instruction based on Galen that had been written hundreds of years earlier by Avicenna. Whatever the choice of textual tinder, there was no way after the St John's Day bonfire to salvage a comfortable, if provocative, academic life in Basel. He later decided to leave town, moving, with a few stops along the way, to the city of Nuremberg, which, like Strasbourg, was a centre of German publishing. There Theophrastus von Hohenheim began to write using a new name, a name expressing an identity that no one else could claim, 'Paracelsus'.

Writing books is one thing, but publishing them is another; and Paracelsus found that, aside from accepting several small pamphlets attacking procedures used to treat syphilis and a few concerning astrological predictions, no publisher was willing to take a chance printing his works. Even before his coming to Nuremberg, the stack of unpublished papers had become substantial. Put simply, what Paracelsus viewed as revolutionary, publishers saw as raising the wrath of the medical establishment, and thus as financially risky. After all, what those papers described was a new medicine (although Paracelsus thought of it as actually being very old): part magic and partly built upon what we would call today observational science, none of it conveying accepted medical opinion. And yet, out of the realms of mysticism, magic, alchemy and concrete experience emerged a conception of the medical art with far-reaching practical consequences. Rather than defining disease as a general imbalance of humours, it described each illness as a distinct entity related to a specific part of the body. Each illness, in other words, had a specific cause and required a specific remedy, and those remedies could be made from any of the parts of nature – animal, vegetable or mineral. Most importantly, this new medicine required knowing how the body worked not just on the basis of anatomy, but on another foundation entirely – namely, chemistry.

What is it, then, that Paracelsus had to say to those who had maligned his theories and practices? How did he explain the need for 'a new medicine'? And, crucially, what did one need to know to practise this medicine knowingly? In both the *Seven Defences* and in an accompanying text included in his *Kärntner Schriften* called *Labyrinthus medicorum errantium* (The Labyrinth of Wandering Physicians) he gave voice to his views and frustrations. Here, in a nutshell, is how he did so.

The Greeks, he acknowledged, had made a great start, but medicine had just not advanced since then. Ancient medicine may have been fine for ancient ailments, but what of today? 'Of what use is the rain that fell a thousand years ago,' he asked.[7] The world was different now. New epochs (he calls them 'monarchies') had come and gone, and with each new epoch, nature herself, and the diseases that afflict humankind, have been a little different. No one got syphilis in the ancient world. Nevertheless, ancient theories about the body and the treatment of illness had become so deeply rooted, so much approved and so well preserved that no one had looked for any sort of an alternative or even considered that the ancient ideas could be wrong. But this was just foolishness, and for the sake of teaching an art that could truly be judged on the basis of how well it worked, he had decided to expose the empty talk of traditional physicians and to trust in what he called the 'light of nature', a kind of revelation that came about through the close examination of natural things.

Paracelsus was a deeply spiritual person. References to biblical passages pepper his medical writings, and as we will see, in many of the writings collected after his death, theology displaced medicine altogether as the focus. The physician, in his view, was a Christ-like figure, a notion long shared in medieval medicine. 'The physician', he writes, 'is he who in the case of bodily illnesses represents [the work of God] and makes God visible.'[8] As Christ had come for the sake of sinners, physicians were there for those who were sick. Yet some physicians had given up on their patients, saying they were incurable. These practitioners had been born from the mother of false medicine, the kind taught at universities. Their ignorance was appalling. 'If you will love your neighbour,' Paracelsus says, 'you must not say: for you there is no help. Rather, you must say: I cannot do it, and I don't understand it [i.e. the art of medicine].' Ancient writings had served more to seduce than to show one the right and straightforward path in medicine. For this reason, he had decided to go it alone and abandon those ideas. He asked the unthinkable: 'how would one learn if there were no books on earth and no physicians at all?' The answer was clear: 'I concluded that medicine could be learned quite well without human teachers.'[9] Instead of reading over and again the books of the ancients, those eager for knowledge had to learn to read different books, and one in particular which had been ignored since ancient days: the book of Nature. In doing that, the physician would refine himself and perfect the art of medicine.

Oddly, Paracelsus and Galen agreed on this point. Art perfected nature and refined those who acquired knowledge of her secrets. All things were improved by art, including the physician. In fact, Galen told the story of the philosopher Diogenes, who, while at a dinner party, all of sudden needed to spit. Diogenes was in the home of a rich man who had collected beautiful things, but who had not paid attention to his own education. Everything in the room – the inlaid floor, the painted murals, the tapestries – demonstrated how it had been perfected by human talent and art. In comparison, the rich householder had been left unrefined. All he had was his money. Diogenes decided, out of respect for the art that had brought such improvement to the world around him, that there was only one suitable place to spit: on his host, the least refined thing in the room.[10]

How did a physician gain improvement? In perfecting the art of medicine through reading the book of Nature, how was 'reading' to be done? The first and most important book to read was the book of wisdom. Since everything in nature comes from God, including medicine, one needed to seek medical knowledge first through prayer. 'This', Paracelsus instructed, 'is the [proper] path to school.'[11] The secrets and mysteries of nature disclosed God's powers in the world, and only through divine grace was one able to open other books that revealed the workings of the firmament and the nature of the elements. True physicians had also to read the book of the greater and lesser worlds. This book described the way that the universe and the human being were interconnected so that the powers of the heavens (the macrocosm) could be condensed within each person (the microcosm). The general idea was ancient and had been given new life by several prominent Renaissance thinkers, but Paracelsus made use of it to argue that the focus of medicine was far greater than the body itself. It was not enough to do what the anatomists did, not enough to observe, cut open, boil and re-inspect the body's parts. This kind of focus, he said, was like that of a peasant who sees a book of psalms but only sees letters without understanding anything more.[12] Paracelsus was after more than that. Medicine was concerned not just with the parts of things, but with the forces that made them function, that made them capable of making and sustaining life. He wanted to know what made the parts come alive. If this reminds us today of Mary Shelley's *Frankenstein*, it is worth noting that, in grappling with the question of how matter gains life, Shelley has Victor Frankenstein, the creature's creator, reading Paracelsus, among others, at the beginning of her wonderful and disquieting story. For Paracelsus, there was only one way to know about the forces that animated the body. When the physician 'understands the greater world, heaven and earth, and all their creations, then he has the knowledge to understand the minor world'.[13] Clearly, the educated physician had a lot to know.

The new medicine that refined the physician also required that doctors learn alchemy. In doing so, they would partake in refining and completing nothing less than the work of creation: 'As all things are created from nothing,' Paracelsus reasoned,

> there is nothing at the beginning that is altogether complete according to its end . . . What is not there entirely the alchemist [*vulcanus*] must complete . . . Thus it is also with medicines; a medicine is created by God, but since nothing is created up to its end, that end is hidden in the dross of things.[14]

To the alchemist–physician the task was given to complete God's work. 'Where the physician cannot do this, he is no doctor, but rather a drunk with a doctor's title, as much like a doctor as an image in the mirror is to a human being.'[15] The practitioner of the new medicine made medicines by his own hand – by knowing how to separate what was pure from what was impure – and thus improved the human condition by lending that hand to the work of the Creator. In doing so, he brought about the fulfilment and purpose of what lay hidden in created things. Paracelsus explained it in the following way:

> Alchemy is that which completes that which has not come to its end . . . As there are alchemists of metals . . . who separate the impure from the pure by means of the fire . . . there are also alchemists of medicine who separate what belongs to a medicine from what does not. So you see what kind of art alchemy is. It is the art of removing the useless from the useful and bringing a thing to its final being and material end.[16]

Finally, and most profoundly, the new medicine required the physician to refine his art by reading and rereading the book called experience. That seems straightforward, but there is a twist, one that is essential to understanding how the world really works. What Paracelsus calls 'experience' we might call theoretical understanding: not just paying attention to the way things happen, but comprehending the reasons why they happen. Experience, in other words, meant something far more than simple observation, no matter how precise. It meant understanding how things knew to do what they did. How did a pear tree 'know' to produce only pears and not some other kind of fruit? What part of nature required it to do so? Knowing this was real experience, the kind of experience that was true learning.

Here is another example, this one in Paracelsus' everyday, earthy language. Both physicians and apothecaries knew, on the basis of common experience, that, when applied to the human body, the plant scammony (*Convolvulus scammonia*) acted as a powerful purgative. 'It does so,' Paracelsus explained, 'with the knowledge that God has given it. [But] if you learn what scammony knows, its knowledge, so that it is in you as it is in scammony, then you know . . . its nature and being.' If you don't, 'then . . . you only know that it makes people shit.'[17] We might think that Paracelsus is simply trying to get at the plant's active principle, but an active principle, for Paracelsus, is just not fundamental enough. We identify such a principle today as glucoside scammonin, or jalapin, a resin that remains inert until it comes into contact with bile in the intestine. Then the bowel reacts – fiercely. But this kind of explanation would have seemed detached from the living world, having no room for the vital powers of the heavens (truly astral powers) that, Paracelsus thought, were communicated to, and compressed within, all the objects of nature. This was the source for the divine plan, or knowledge, within things, a knowledge that existed also in the human being and made it possible for the human being to listen in on nature's secrets. That cosmic rapport drove learnt experience and separated it from the everyday sort. It also made a physician's medical know-how truly credible.

> If one says: 'do [that], I have often tried it', this is . . . [what I call] experience without knowledge. Don't place your trust in such a person . . . However, whoever possesses experience with knowledge, that person is someone you can trust . . . From this it follows that each person should advance God's gift and knowledge, which is in him, to the highest level by means of alchemy.[18]

So, key to the new kind of medicine that Paracelsus constructs, and which many of his contemporary doctors detested, is the idea that the powers of the macrocosm are wrapped up in the stuff of which terrestrial things are made. This is what the physician who was truly experienced in the new medicine had to know. Defying ancient ideas about the fundamental elements of terrestrial things, Paracelsus also rejected the notion that all things in the immediate physical world were composed of earth, air, fire and water. In his view, there was something that preceded even them: the cosmological wombs, as he called them, of Sulphur, Salt and Mercury. These were known as the 'first three' (*tria prima*); they produced each body, sensitive as well as insensitive, metals and minerals, as well as herbs, plants, animals and people. The knowledge of powers – of how things knew what to do, and what they could be expected to do when applied as medicines – was, therefore, chemical at its root. This is where the new medicine staked out a new frontier. The human being was a divinely created, spiritually infused, chemical apparatus. The body worked in an alchemical way. Its parts possessed their own 'inner alchemist' that 'knew' how to separate what was useful to the body from what was not. They 'knew' how to circulate, sublimate and distil. 'For these arts,' Paracelsus declared, 'are all in the human being, as [they are] also in the alchemy of the outer world.'[19]

No wonder traditional doctors hated him. Their medicine was nothing like this. Paracelsus was sure, however, that their condemnations would ring hollow, since they had very little to show for all their art. 'The question is', he says, 'whether the doctrine of the university physician is the art of medicine, or whether mine is. That will be proven by means of works.'[20] He might just as well have said, 'my art will be proven correct as it succeeds better in curing the sick.' After all, he argues elsewhere, 'as the master, so the pupil, as the smith, so the arms, as the art, so the works.'[21] The works and practices of traditional physicians led to the abandonment of the sick when the going got tough. The true physician, however, never turned his back on his neighbour, but conveyed 'great love and good will to all the sick', secure in the truths conveyed by learnt experience and mindful that, in the art of medicine, 'God dwells and works therein.'[22]

TWO

Seeing through the Body: Nature, Disease and What the True Physician Must Know

Of the children born into the world that Paracelsus knew, many were dead before they reached two or three years old. Infant mortality was so high, in fact, that the average age in the early sixteenth century was around thirty years. Not everybody died young, of course, and some certainly led long and satisfying lives. With some good fortune to allow them to escape the ravages of war, pandemic and famine, some people might live to see seventy, eighty or even years beyond – though, by then, their children would most likely be dead, and probably their grandchildren, too.

This chapter deals with both Paracelsus' struggle to redefine disease and the tempest occasioned by his introduction of a new way to know the body. Next to responding to the accusation that he had created a new medicine, in the second of his *Seven Defences*, Paracelsus needed to answer to the charge that he had needlessly created new names for diseases. In response, he argued that different names were necessary because the older medicine was wrong in the way that it had described the origin of diseases, and thus in the way that it had addressed their cures. Making use of books written two thousand years before had accomplished so little, he said, that an unschooled peasant was able to heal better than supposedly learned physicians with all their books and red-hooded robes.[1] There were, moreover, new diseases to be confronted that the ancients had never known. How was one to explain that?

Disease was, and is, part of life, and traditional physicians frequently practised the diagnosis of disease without ever seeing their patients, reaching conclusions on the basis of letters or written reports. One of the most common methods of diagnosis was by means of examining urine. Was it salty or sweet to the taste? Was it cloudy, clear, with or without sediment? And, especially, what was its colour? In this regard, colour charts helped physicians pinpoint excesses of humours. Troublesome humours were one thing; troublesome patients were another, and some were known to send in the urine of animals or of another person, to test a physician's skill. If a patient appeared in person, the attending physician first paid attention to external appearances, especially the combinations of hot, cold, wet and dry, to identify which humours were out of balance.

There were also particular procedures for identifying specific illnesses. A popular guide gave instructions about observing blood drawn from the patient. Was it thick or thin? Was it hot, cold, greasy or foamy? Into what layers did it separate and how quickly did it congeal? If blood felt greasy after having coagulated and been washed, this was bad news: the patient had leprosy. Sometimes physicians attempted diagnoses on the basis of touch. A specific sound made by the abdomen when percussed might indicate dropsy (an accumulation of fluid). Abscesses and tumours felt like a hard mass, and some physicians thought that the pulse was a kind of code of the body, signalling its condition by means of rhythm, strength and a variety of subtle indications.

Some illnesses could be described only in general terms – oppression of the liver or spleen, diseases of the chest and so on. But other complaints were easy to recognize: headaches, toothaches, haemorrhoids, bladder or kidney stones, for instance. Recognizing and treating fevers had a literature of its own. Illnesses that were self-limiting required forbearance and were usually treated by means of changes in diet or by taking medications aimed at reducing symptoms. Others might require surgery – always as a last resort. Where illness and pain were commonplace, and where regimens of treatment also required the endurance of discomfort, what counted as an affliction must have been reserved for the most severe suffering. In any case, it was best to remain fatalistic. Physicians could only do so much, after all. At a certain point, there was nothing else to be expected from medicine. Only prayer and divine intercession remained.

The ancient Roman Stoic philosopher Seneca recalled that Alexander the Great had once begun to study geometry. 'Poor fellow,' he wrote, 'inasmuch as he would thus find out how minute the earth really was, the earth of which he had possessed himself of a tiny part.' How could he call himself 'Great' with such a small claim to fame?[2] True, some things gain a different significance by comparison, but there was nothing to compare with the experience of mass death brought to Europe in the mid-fourteenth century by a disease that the ancient world seemingly did not know – the plague. We think of it now as bubonic plague, a catch-all reference to what probably was a combination of diseases making up a series of pandemics entangling bubonic, pneumatic and septicaemic plague. Researchers point to a Genoese fleet that landed in the Sicilian harbour of Messina in 1347 carrying the disease to Europe, but to those enduring its presence, its origins were obscure. Some blamed 'bad air'. Some blamed an alignment of planets. Some thought in terms of divine punishment. Others blamed lepers, Muslims or Jews. Whatever its cause, the effect was catastrophic. Some cities lost the majority of their population. Some villages vanished altogether. Physicians thought in terms of morbid seeds, or tiny fragments, of disease, or assumed that the air had been made putrid by an excess of heat and moisture, by vapours emitted from the earth's interior, or by the exhalations of those dying of the disease. Plague, like leprosy, was thought to be contagious, and only distance gave a small measure of protection. Changing the air with fumigations might keep bad air away, but physicians had little to offer and many simply fled, leaving resolute surgeons and determined city councils to deal with the terrifying reality of persistent mass death. Neither was plague, in its various forms, ever really over, as it continued to cause havoc in one place or another throughout Europe for centuries thereafter. The fifteenth century endured 41 years of plague; the sixteenth suffered through thirty.

Syphilis (the name first appeared in 1530) was another newcomer and was often confused with leprosy. Both were viewed as weaving together sin and contagion. In the case of leprosy, some thought that arousal and stimulation through intercourse made the body more receptive to the poisonous exhalations of an infected partner. In the case of syphilis, genital symptoms indicated venereal origins. Syphilis was a big problem: for the period between 1524 and 1532, a worker at Strasbourg's 'General Charity' recorded the presence of 411 sick poor: 196 women, 164 men and 51 children. Among them, the largest number were cases of syphilis (254 cases) (illus. 6). At Nuremberg, his new home for a time after leaving Basel, Paracelsus turned his attention to this disease and struggled to get several works concerning syphilis into print. An essay concerning the symptoms of the disease had already come together shortly before, while he made a stopover in Colmar, a thriving market town in the upper Rhine valley situated between the Low Countries and Switzerland. In Nuremberg, two additional tracts by Paracelsus appeared around 1529 – a short essay and a lengthier tract attacking conventional cures, including the use of mercury (internally and externally) and treatments (usually fumigations) involving a wood imported from the West Indies called *Guaiacum* (illus. 7). For a time, this wood was a sought-after remedy, so much so that a practitioner treating patients at Strasbourg's 'General Charity' documented needing to buy two 'zentner' and 15 pounds (over 100 kilograms) of it at the Frankfurt fair.[3] A third tract never made it through the print shop door, its publication quashed by a medical establishment alarmed at having been accused of causing more harm than good. Paracelsus attempted to respond with another book, whose publication was blocked and which did not appear in print until after his death. The book, called *Paragranum*, was written in the months between 1529 and 1530 in the little town of Beratzhausen after he had left Nuremberg and its physicians behind. It was a comprehensive introduction to his medical

ANDREAE ALCIATI

Nupta contagioso.

Dij meliora pijs, Mezenti. cur age sic me
Compellas? emptus quòd tibi dote gener,
Gallica quem scabies, dira & mentagra perurit.
Hoc est quidnam aliud, dic mihi sæue pater,
Corpora corporibus quàm iungere mortua uiuis,
Efferáq; Etrusci facta nouare ducis?

6 Syphilis imagined as an ancient torture of tying a corpse to a living person, illustration from *Andreae Alciati emblematum frontes quatuor* (1531).

philosophy and it carried a preface, written with scatological references and rhetorical venom, aimed at settling the score with those who had chastised his teachings and had prevented the printed circulation of his ideas.

Outwardly, Paracelsus argued, university physicians made a pretty picture, but inwardly they amounted to nothing more than shit handlers and painted idols. He had exposed their errors, and because of that, he had been mocked and humiliated. They had called him 'Cacophrastus', but their medicine was a swindle and the language they used gibberish. They concealed their lies behind the theory of humours, but this Cacophrastus would now make the common man their judge. With his own medical alchemy, he would boil away their Asclepius, Avicenna and Galen; he would burn them up until nothing was left but their dregs. They had labelled

7 Treatment of syphilis with a preparation of guaiac (*Guaiacum*) wood. The mirror reflects the sexual origin of the disease. Engraving from *Nova reperta* by Phillip Galle (1537–1612) after Stradanus.

him an outcast of their universities, a heretic and seducer of students, but he knew that their purgations, cauteries, cuttings and burnings were impostures. He had been called the 'Luther of physicians' and knew that the same crowd hated him as they hated the religious reformer, wishing for them both the punishment of eternal fire.

Luther could take care of himself, Paracelsus wrote, and he would defend himself against the physicians who had attacked him. That, he added, would be easy, since his opponents lacked the kind of learnt experience that he possessed. He wished he could protect his own bald head from the flies as easily as he could defend himself against those who mocked him. Was he less worthy because he was not dressed in their professional attire? Should he be less acceptable because he held no office and had not been received into the courts of princes? After all, it was God who made good physicians, not popes, emperors or universities. He had tried to serve princes and peasants alike, and in doing so had come to know more than all the scribes of the old medicine. His shoestrings, he said, were more learned than their Galen and Avicenna. His beard had more experience than their universities. He looked forward to the time when all those who condemned him would be dragged around by pigs. His name was Theophrastus, not Cacophrastus, and they could eat the same shit they had dished out in ridiculing his name. So how did they like their Cacophrastus now? How did they like their 'forest donkey from Einsiedeln'? Not one of them would be found upon whom the dogs would not shit.[4]

Such rhetoric might have been cathartic for Paracelsus, but his real message and purpose lay ahead. If the old medicine was false and good for nothing, what were the foundations of the true medical art? The true physician, he declared, needed to be experienced in four things, which he called the four pillars of medicine: philosophy, astronomy, alchemy and virtue. He was quick to point out that in studying nature, nothing should ever be so firmly established that it could not be questioned, and nothing so questionable that it could not possibly have a claim to truth. The ancient philosopher Aristotle (384–322 BC) was the villain here. His philosophy had risen to the top of academic learning like scum in a pot, obscuring what was good underneath. From this scum-philosophy had arisen the scum-physician. What Aristotle covered up, Paracelsus argued, was an older truth, an even more ancient philosophy, one that revealed the occult powers that linked the heavens and the earth. This philosophy concerned itself with the hidden forces of nature and joined the human being (the microcosm) to the heavens (the macrocosm). The true physician studied the microcosm by studying the heavens and, conversely, learnt about the heavens by also studying the human body. When one understood the microcosm in the external world, one would also comprehend the wonders and secret things of the world that resided in the human being. 'The occult powers of the earthly firmament are disclosed to the physician,' Paracelsus wrote. 'To him alone are the occult powers of nature made manifest.'[5]

Studying the heavens meant studying their influences, and the celestial powers that connected the human body to the heavenly bodies Paracelsus called *astra*. These powers worked through the elements to bring about generation and change. So the physician studied astronomy to comprehend the powers of celestial *astra* and the ways in which they operated upon the body beneficially – maintaining the health and function of its parts – and harmfully, as a source of disease. Disease, in other words, was not something outside nature, not some other order of thing, nor was it nature gone wrong. Disease was part of nature, part of the intelligence of nature; it was that part of nature that knows how things should be when things fall apart, as everything must. Disease is the intelligence by which the body knows to be sick, to fall apart a little or a lot, in one way rather than another. It is also the reason why the way we fall apart is constantly changing. Whatever proceeds through time is subject to the powers of the heavens, and over time those powers change, having different effects upon different earthly places. So the physician must be an astronomer, observing the external heavens as a guide to the knowledge of the internal heavens of the body. In this way, what is otherwise invisible becomes visible.

Alchemy was another of the pillars of medicine because alchemy guided the celestial powers and brought about specific changes in the world. The alchemy of nature turned grass into milk, made wine out of earth and was the reason pears ripened. Alchemy was another way of recognizing what was invisible within the visible world. If one knew nothing about alchemy, one could know nothing about the *mysteria* of nature, the plentiful virtues and powers that resided in things. More importantly alchemy was the way that the human being got involved in completing the work of creation. Nature, Paracelsus proclaimed,

> brings nothing to light that is complete as it stands. Rather, the human being must perfect [its substances].

> This completion is called *alchimia*. For the alchemist is the baker in baking bread, the vintner in making the wine, the weaver in weaving cloth. Thus, whatever arises out of nature for human use is brought to that condition ordained by nature by an alchemist.[6]

All of nature (the macrocosm as well as the microcosm) worked alchemically. The creation itself, which began as a separation of light from darkness, was in constant alchemical motion. From an initial *mysterium magnum* (great or divine mystery), an alchemical process of separation brought into being the three fundamental principles of Sulphur, Salt and Mercury. These *tria prima* gave rise to the elements from which everything in the world – whether animal, vegetable or mineral – was formed. As a gigantic alchemical vessel, says Paracelsus, the heavens themselves 'cook, digest, imbibe, resolve, and reverberate in every direction, just as does the alchemist'.[7]

The body worked by means of alchemy as well, each part containing an internal alchemist that directed the powers of the world (the *astra*) towards a specific purpose or function. In this way, each part of the body knew what to do. We think today of the role of DNA, whose genes provide the messages that assemble or alter the body's proteins, the means by which the body does things. For Paracelsus, the internal alchemist also had the job of separating what was useful from what was not in the body. Since the influences of the greater world, the *astra*, also contained disease, the internal alchemist needed to separate what was poisonous from what was beneficial to the body. So it would be far too limiting if one should say, 'alchemy makes only gold or silver'. Its real purpose was to reveal the divine secrets of nature (arcana) and especially to make medicines with which to treat disease. So the physician needed to understand the processes by which alchemists worked. He or she needed to know what calcination and sublimation were and needed to understand distillation and fermentation, because these processes were the means by which all chemical natures were completed, as much in the realm of minerals and metals as in the body. Knowing these things allowed the physician to come to the aid of the body's 'internal alchemist', the ability of the body to separate what was useful from what was not. The two, the body and the physician, then worked together, the 'internal alchemist' receiving help from the physician–alchemist, who supplied, by laboratory means, what a specific part of the body required. Making medicines and applying them in this manner, Paracelsus knew, would be controversial. 'Whether the universities follow me or not is not up to me,' he wrote,

> But do not despise my writings and be turned from them because I am solitary, because I am new, or because I am German. For it is in this way that the art of medicine must proceed and be learned and no other.[8]

Terrible things were concealed in medicine as it had been established and practised, and Paracelsus pointed to murder, mayhem, mutilation, corruption, exploitation, theft and plunder as just its most noticeable depravities. For this reason, a fourth 'pillar' was necessary to support the true physician, one that emphasized the role of virtue in medical practice. Put simply, or perhaps not so simply, the physician must learn to imitate Christ and to play a Christ-like role in being useful to others and not to himself. False physicians, like false prophets, apostles, martyrs and confessors, liked to say, 'We are from God. Look what we can do . . . Look how God works through us.' But how was it Christ-like, Paracelsus asked, for physicians to steal the property of their patients, taking away even their houses, eating up everything a man possessed, leaving his family stripped bare? God had created the art of medicine, but being indifferent to truth had led some physicians to buy their medical degrees so as to adorn themselves with titles, as if to say 'I am so noble! I am a doctor!' Christ was absent here. Look at the pride, luxury and ostentation in the way they live, he instructed. Look at their wives, adorned in golden chains, giving them the appearance of nobility. The real physician, he declared, performs the works of God and is in no way given over to such lust, pride or cunning. Rather than reading a few books in preparation for his art, this real physician pursues learning and experience from youth to old age and thereby comes to recognize the working of divine powers embedded in creation.[9] Ironically, outside the Christian context, the ancient physician Galen would have agreed, for the most part. The real physician, Galen believed, must despise money. The best doctor, he thought, was also a philosopher and would thus not only know how to evaluate evidence, but would be disinterested in glorifying himself, having an interest only in the improvement of his art.

When defending himself against those who charged him with having invented new diseases and given them new names, Paracelsus argued that the ideas of physicians rooted in the ancient theory of humours could not adequately explain how 'new' diseases, especially pandemics, occurred. In his view, diseases were in a constant state of flux, coming about or appearing in specific locations as a result of the natural processes of a changing world. In this way, Paracelsus made disease itself part of the terrain of history. New diseases came into being as part of historical time. The heavens, the macrocosm, acted differently every day. 'The reason', he explained, is that 'it too is getting older'. Like a child, the heavens had a beginning, and, like an adult, it will have its death. Everything changes with age, and as things age, their actions change too.

Nature is never fixed, and the causes of disease are affected by changes in place and time. The skilled physician needed to pay attention to such changes, but in accounting for diseases in this historical way, a new language was required, one that would allow for an up-to-date connection between the objects of a changing world and their description. Moreover, Paracelsus observed, the conditions of life had also changed. Never before had so many people, from so many different places, come to live together. Probably thinking of the scourge of syphilis, he noted further that 'the human commerce in fleshy lusts' had never been as it is now for 'as long as the world has existed'.[10]

Besides syphilis, Paracelsus described in the late 1520s the origins, causes and symptoms of a number of other diseases, in particular epilepsy, dropsy, gout and jaundice. And in the early 1530s he composed one of the first texts focused upon occupational disease, in this case a description of illnesses associated with mining. Here the focus was upon diseases of the lung – including consumption – and illnesses associated with metal poisoning. Along the way, he further developed ideas about a specific kind of disease – one that, given the general occurrence of dehydration, must have been one of the most frequent and most painful experiences of illness in the Renaissance era. He called them 'tartarous illnesses'; today we call them bladder or kidney stones, being the formation of calculi, usually mineral salts, in the ducts of particular organs (most often the bladder or kidneys, but also in other places). The discussion of 'tartarous illness' was already present in Paracelsus' lectures at Basel. It retained a strong presence within his writings thereafter and finally found a formalized place as *Das Buch von den tartarischen Krankheiten* (The Book of Tartarous Illnesses), appearing alongside his *Septem defensiones* and the *Labyrinthus medicorum errantium*; in the *Kärntner Schriften*.

Where Hippocrates had explained the presence of stones in the body as being a result of coagulated phlegm, Paracelsus attributed its formation to 'tartar'. Tartar arose from the fatty parts of food or drink, and some foods and some drinks were worse than others. Beer contained a lot of mucus and formed tartar in the stomach. However, drinking warm beer with butter (which was slippery) helped send the sticky part of the beer on its way. Milk and cheese were tartaric as well. If the stomach, liver and kidneys separated what was pure in them from what was impure, there was no problem. But when these parts were weak, what was impure and not well separated became a kind of mucus that gradually turned stony. When it became a sand, Paracelsus called it tartar.[11] Even some waters produced tartaric stuff, and Paracelsus referred to the Emperor Friedrich, who tested the water he drank by comparing the weight of a cloth left to dry after being dunked into well water with the weight of the original cloth. The difference, Paracelsus thought, was the amount of tartar contained in the water.[12]

When stones occurred, treatment required dissolving the tartaric mass. Paracelsus prescribed white tartar – we call it potassium bitartrate, or cream of tartar. It was easy to acquire in quantity as it could be scraped off the inside of wine casks (indeed, some will also know it as 'wine diamonds', the crystals that form on corks in wine bottles). Regardless of where it came from, Paracelsus thought of it as a stony material that would grind to pieces the tartaric stones formed in the body.

According to Paracelsus, stomach ailments and virtually all fevers were connected to the presence of tartar. As tartar putrefied in the stomach, it became a subtle and penetrating air, causing colic and a twisting of the flesh. Fevers arising in the kidneys, he thought, came from putrefied tartar. Some also rose from the stomach and liver, but the fevers in the kidneys were the most severe. Women, however, endured a special misery. Liquid tartar, along with bile, could press from the stomach, where digestion was ruined, and into the uterus, twisting it to such an extent that infertility followed. In such cases, pains were so burning and persistent that Paracelsus recommended pills of laudanum (a tincture of opium) to help with the spasms.[13] Tartar also interfered with reproduction. When mixed with the male seed, it could cause miscarriages. Paracelsus recommended that women be cleansed, after conception, with a preparation of mugwort (probably *Artemesia vulgaris*).[14]

The experience of pain, even acute pain of the stony sort, is subjective and, as such, is hard to define and harder still to evaluate. Nonetheless, Paracelsus prescribed medicines and regimens aimed at stemming pain. Relaxing by means of laudanum preparations may have helped to reduce the pain endured in passing urinary calculi, but to treat the cause of illness, physicians needed to know where diseases came from. This leads us to one of the most interesting and curious facets of Paracelsus' medical philosophy that is described in a particular writing called *Das Buch paramirum* (The Book beyond Wonder). Paracelsus scholars have to be careful to distinguish this book from another with a very similar title called *Opus paramirum* (A Work beyond Wonder). Where the latter concerned itself substantially with the first matter of heaven and earth (matter Paracelsus called *limbus*) and with the doctrine of the creative principles (Sulphur, Salt and Mercury), *Das Buch paramirum* focused on the question of why there is disease at all and how to explain its origins.

What must have rocked the medical establishment at its very footings was the idea that, although the body experienced illness, the body was really not to blame. To locate the cause of illness, one had to look outside, not inside, the body. Disease arose not from bodily humours or from within the anatomy of the body's parts, but, he said, from five 'beings' or 'powers' that connected each person to a specific environment in an ever-changing cosmological order. Remember, the macrocosm and the microcosm are one and the same, and everything in nature falls apart – these powers accounted for why the body did so. There was no avoiding their influence, but the medical practitioner who recognized their origin and potency could, nevertheless, intervene with effective treatments and forestall their effects. The true physician could look through the human being and find the origin of disease in the operations of nature.

Given the connection between the macrocosm and microcosm, it comes as no surprise that the first power is an astral being, or *ens astrale*.[15] While for Paracelsus the heavenly bodies do not have powers that can shape a person's character, they do nevertheless cause disease as part of the ecology of human existence. We live with both, and cannot live without them. From the heavens come the powers that sustain life in every form. However, 'the stars have their natures and their various characteristics just like people on earth,' and sometimes they are just maliciously disposed.[16] In those cases, what emanates from them is a poison, and this poison pollutes the air, producing in specific regions a vapour that, if a person is not well fortified against it or is in a weakened condition, creates disease. The cosmic kitchen is continually producing changes in the chemical make-up of the physical world, altering the chemical equilibrium within a particular location or individual. Parts of the heavens produce too much acid. Other parts produce too much arsenic, sulphur, salt or mercury. When this happens diseases are sure to follow, their kind dependent upon the chemical constitution of the individual and the specific region where he or she lives.

Another source of what is poisonous to the body is the very food or drink that sustains our lives. Everything taken into the body can both nurture and corrupt. Everything contains a poisonous being, an *ens veneni* that penetrates all of nature.[17] The animals and fruits of the earth are in themselves neither food nor poison, but become so only when consumed. Then it is the job of the internal alchemist to separate what is good from what is bad and convert that which is imperfect into something useful to life. In this way, for Paracelsus, illness is part of the experience of life, just as poison is part of the environment; and death is not only inevitable, but essential to being here at all.

The implicit message here is that it is not nature's aim to sustain our lives. Nature does not care what happens to us. The twentieth-century French philosopher and physician Georges Canguilhem (1904–1995) observed that 'if we delegate the task of restoring the diseased organism to the desired norm by technical means, either magical or matter of fact . . . it is because we expect nothing good from nature itself.'[18] Modern medicine is largely biotechnology, and the assumption is that no one really need die if the right technology can be found and applied. Paracelsus would have recognized the illusion and would have reminded us that human existence is, in itself, pathological. Being alive means to be poisoned daily, at least to the extent that by living we are constantly involved with an environment that is to us contaminated, although to itself, it is just nature. Death and disease, as categories of the everyday, are not things 'out there', different from life, to be kept at a distance and at bay. They are rather aspects of life, intimate with living.

For Paracelsus, nature thus contained both good and bad, and the chemical processes (fermentation, digestion, distillation and so on) in the body – what Paracelsus called the 'inner alchemist' – separated the harmful from the useful. But sometimes the inner alchemist fails to function as it should, and then another process, namely putrefaction, or decay – already there by nature – begins to run the show, and disease follows. As he writes, 'every putrefaction poisons the site in which it occurs and is the hearth of a certain deadly poison,' just as it also becomes the seat for those diseases that are subject to it.[19]

Diseases of a third sort arose from what Paracelsus called a 'natural power', the *ens naturale*.[20] These are illnesses that relate to one's own individual constitution, one's own specifically constructed micro-firmament. As the outer world contains good things and bad, so this world also contains the constellations of both health and corruption. No matter where you go, in other words, you have to take your own little world along, and sometimes, no matter how pleasant or normal the day, this ruins everything, as you get sick and no one else does.

Have you ever noticed that, sometimes, you get sick of people and that some people just make you sick? Paracelsus summed up his ideas about that sort of thing by referring to diseases belonging to a disease category that he called the spiritual being, *ens spirituale* – illnesses related to the spiritual or emotional side of life.[21] These are ailments often arising from personal and social relationships and that reflect what some today would call emotional or psychosomatic illness. Each of us possesses a spiritual life or consciousness, and Paracelsus is careful to say that when referring to this, he is not referring to something theological. This is nothing that stems from Christian belief. There is no devil involved, he says. This is really the work of the mind – the spiritual part of the body. Spirit and body are so intertwined, however, that the one can make the other sick. When the spirit suffers, the body also suffers.

There may be little surprise here. In a world of stress and depression – and their well-known physical consequences – most of us no longer think in terms of the dualism of mind and body, but rather of a unity, mind–body. The truly interesting thing, however, is that, in Paracelsus' view, one spirit can affect another, making another spirit–body relationship sick. Think of what happens to others when we use language, Paracelsus explains: words go forth, and sometimes they please, but sometimes words hurt.

> Just as the word goes out, so does the spirit which has his abode in conformity with what we will and desire . . . if I should desire with a will having one purpose to injure someone else, this will is a creature of my spirit. My spirit, therefore, will, according to my pleasure, act against the spirit I have in view . . . For you and your mind are one . . . [In this case] take care not to treat the body with medicines. For that would be in vain. However, treat the mind, and the body will get well.[22]

Paracelsus realized that the effects of emotion, of desire and of will were important to medical treatment. He also knew that, for some, this would be yet another idea that would be hard to take:

> And don't you physicians treat this as a joke; you are not aware of the smallest part that the power of the will plays. For the will is the matrix of such spirits as are not under the jurisdiction of reason . . . The hand can injure a man without touching him. Likewise the tongue hits him with words whom you have in mind. It should be clear that all this takes place through a medium, and by the power of spirit.[23]

So, the mind can make oneself, or someone else, sick. The cure is not medication but a change of emotion – and most useful of all is love. Once again, the little physician from Einsiedeln ends up at the centre of a controversy that rages still today: can love and companionship help sustain well-being and, when necessary, make one well again? Holistic medicine says even cancer can be treated in this way. Materialists, of course, think such claims absurd. Over the years, the pendulum has swung one way and then the other. For a very long time, at least until the 1880s, melancholy, depression and grief were thought to be significant factors in the onset of cancer. For the Austrian philosopher, social reformer and founder of the anthroposophic movement, Rudolf Steiner (1861–1925), Paracelsus' notions of an astral connection in the body and of a mind–body unity were alive and well. Feeling and will in the spiritual body corresponded to nerves, the respiratory system and the metabolism in the physical body. Others, like the physicians Georg Groddeck (1866–1934), Viktor von Weizsäcker (1866–1957) and Richard Siebeck (1883–1965) went further, pioneering and further defining German psychosomatic medicine.

Not all believed that disease followed from psychic dispositions, but most held that personal conflicts often materialized themselves as physical ailments. Most dramatic in this regard were the views of another physician, Wilhelm Kütemeyer (1904–1972), who linked cancer to the feelings created by inner conflicts arising from submissive attitudes to authority. Others within the psychosomatic movement rejected the view, but emotions continued to be placed centre stage by psychoanalysts and others when dealing with questions of disease etiology. As the concept of stress gained attention in the 1940s and '50s, attending to pent-up emotions related to conflicts in social life became another way of addressing the issue, and many practitioners accepted, whether they knew it or not, an implicit Paracelsian message: that if emotions did not directly cause diseases, they could, when used therapeutically, be very useful in treating them.[24]

Finally, Paracelsus introduces a disease category called the *ens Dei*, whereby he acknowledges that all diseases come from God.[25] As we will see, Paracelsus knew the Bible and sacred texts well enough to be regarded as a lay preacher by some. In his religious thinking as well as in his medical writings, the concept of providence plays a central role. In the *ens Dei*, it is providence, illustrating the power of God through an unfolding divine plan, that predestines the appearance and course of each disease. God is the ultimate author, in other words, of human happiness and misery, and disease exists in the redemptive context of guilt and repentance as a personal purgatory, a punishment enacted upon an evil world. To every thing, there is a season, and to every disease, there is a certain time in which God allows healing to take place. Each disease, then, must be healed in accordance with what is predestined by God, and Paracelsus acknowledged that this was getting more difficult all the time, since the evil in the world had become steadily worse. When Hippocrates and Galen were alive, it was, he says, pure pleasure to practise medicine. Purgatory on earth (as disease) was then a small affair. Things were worse now, with more evil in the world and many more bad physicians. Some diseases were so bad that even good physicians could not stop them. Only faith in Christ, the arch-physician, could help in such cases. But in the end, even though the methods and practices of the real physician come from God, all efforts are predetermined to fail. 'Then, all illnesses will cease, and such a great change will take place that no illness is present any longer, having changed like white into black.'[26] It is then that what always has been, will be also for us, as we join death.

THREE

The Alchemy of Things in the Making: Medicines as Poisons and Poisons as Medicines

f you were browsing in German bookshops in the 1530s, near the time when Paracelsus was writing his *Paramirum* and *Paragranum*, you would have found many books referring to 'alchemy'. Some of those books would have described traditional views about the origins of metals and minerals in the earth. Some of them would have discussed, on the solid basis of ancient natural philosophy, the transmutation of metals. Some would have been more concerned with making medicines. A few would have described nature in spiritual terms, promising to reveal magical secrets derived from ancient sages. Alchemy mattered in the Renaissance and early modern era, attracting the attention of both lay and learned. On the one hand, it expressed itself as an erudite subject defined within the boundaries of textual traditions arising from ancient authorities and modified by medieval and Renaissance scholars. On the other, however, it existed within a less formal milieu as the province of artisans and craftsmen and thus survived within the realm of everyday practice and private life.

As you browsed, you might have stopped to look at one book claiming to instruct the reader in the *Proper Use of Alchemy*.

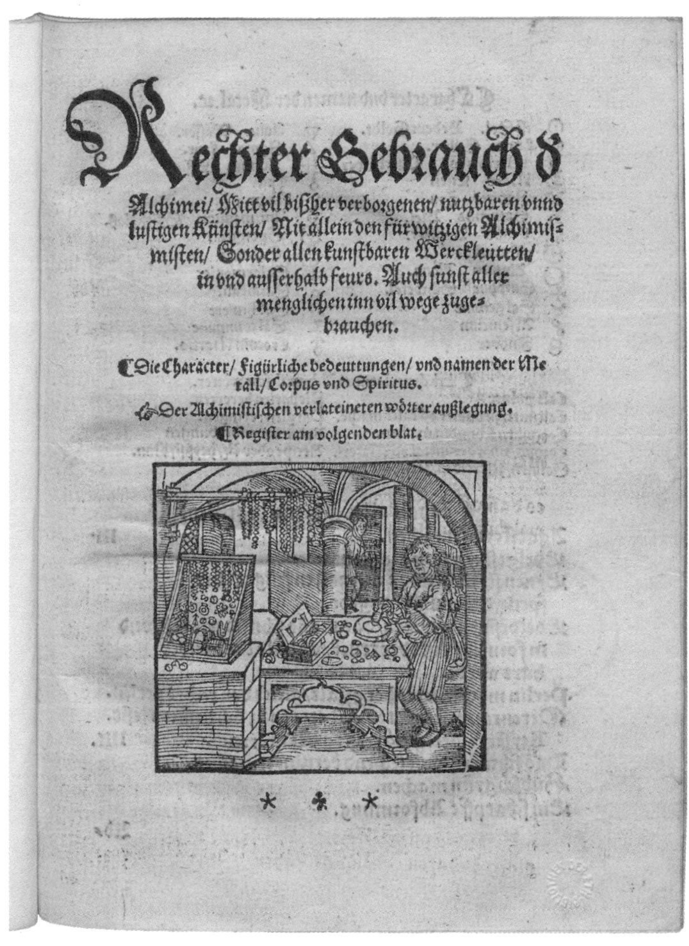

Rechter Gebrauch d

Alchimei/ Mitt vil bißher verborgenen/ nutzbaren vnnd lustigen Künsten/ Nit allein den fürwitzigen Alchimisten/ Sonder allen kunstbaren Wercklеutten/ in vnd ausserhalb feurs. Auch sunst aller menglichen inn vil wege zugebrauchen.

Die Character/ Figürliche bedeuttungen/ vnd namen der Metall/ Corpus vnd Spiritus.

Der Alchimistischen verlateineten wörter außlegung.

Register am volgenden blat.

* ♣ *

You would note the rather nice title page and the promises to reveal something about the hidden and very useful procedures known to inquiring alchemists (illus. 8). When we look at this book today, we may not recognize the figure in the picture as an alchemist as he is not represented doing what most of us expect alchemists to do. He is not conjuring the

8 Title page from *Rechter Gebrauch d'Alchimei* (The Proper Use of Alchemy, 1531).

philosophers' stone or decoding secret symbols. He is making and selling earrings, bracelets and necklaces. That disconnection between what we expect and what we find when we look is culturally telling. When we are surprised like this we are reminded that there is sometimes a big difference between the historical world as it has been described to us and the one in which people really lived. The alchemist in the picture is not representing a knowledge of symbolic mysteries; in fact, he is not representing mystical insight or a belief about anything in particular. He is an alchemist not because of divine revelation or a privileged knowledge of ancient, inscrutable secrets. He is an alchemist because of something he does, something that he knows how to make.

That alchemy was an activity practised by many people for ordinary reasons is not the common image of alchemy we have today. What usually springs to mind is the pursuit of metallic transmutation, especially changing base metals into gold. There was some of that, but most in the sixteenth century recognized that alchemical work encompassed a great deal more. A famous mathematician and physician named Gerolamo Cardano (1501–1576), a contemporary of Paracelsus, gives us a nice description of the different kinds of things practised by those involved with what he called the *ars chymistica* (the chymistic art).

Cardano was a prolific writer who had a tough life. His travails, recorded in an autobiography, began even before he was born. Cardano's mother took several concoctions in an attempt to abort her unborn son. Nothing worked, and what she could not do on her own, plague almost did for her. The disease killed Gerolamo's three half-brothers and it struck him too shortly after his birth. He survived, alive but disfigured. Among the numerous books that he wrote in his 75-year lifetime was one that appeared in 1551 in which he described the *ars chymistica* – not in terms of theories or principles, but as things that artisans knew how to make by bringing about changes to nature. In other words, he just knew the art when he saw it.

The things he observed practitioners being able to produce were myriad. They knew how to stretch glass into long strands and interweave glass with white threads. What Cardano is describing is called 'filigrano'. When you add tin oxide to glass you get a milky glass that was called *lattimo*. In the sixteenth century, craftsmen manipulated white canes of *lattimo*, pressing them into hot glass to make different patterns, or *filigrana*, usually stripes, spirals or twists. They also knew how to make false gems and artificial amber, and how to engrave images into glass. They mixed, altered and refined metals. They made white gold, or electrum. They produced waters and oils by means of distillations and extractions with alcohol, and they knew how to construct the instruments of distillation. Especially, they could create 'dissolving waters' capable of penetrating spaces (and thus able to separate substances) judged impossible when left to their own specific natures. Practitioners of this art, in other words, were especially good at making acids. They made sulphuric acid (called oil of vitriol) by burning sulphur with saltpetre; produced hydrochloric acid (called *aqua regia*) from vitriol and common salt; and made nitric acid (*aqua fortis*), which they used for dissolving metals, especially silver (but not gold), by distilling green vitriol with saltpetre and alum.

They also knew some tricks. They bleached silk and whitened flowers by means of sulphuric vapours, for instance; and they knew secrets of a very practical nature. They made pigments, inks and cosmetics; produced hardened stones; and knew how to soften bone and horn to make a variety of useful things like handles, sword hilts and combs. This was an art that appeared not as a result of speculations about why nature did things, but as a result of understanding well enough how nature worked in order to make things oneself. Some of these things, Cardano says, are admirable, some worthless, some dubious, some beautiful; some aided health and some, he had to admit, were divine. One such dubious thing was making gold. The odds were better for making silver, but this was still, he thought, a long shot.

Like Paracelsus, Cardano was critical of the medical establishment. But since he was himself a university-trained physician, he was criticized as a medical insider. One of Cardano's earliest books, published in 1536 and for the most part written while he was still a student, was called *De malo recentiorum medicorum medendi usu libellus* (Concerning the Bad Practices of Modern Physicians). In it, he rebuked 72 specific practices of physicians and was especially critical of their understanding of the preparation and use of medicaments. Making medicines had become a tool of greed. Many physicians prescribed them when they were unnecessary, as in cases of childhood epilepsy or for minor illnesses, or when medicaments were of no use, as in cases of hectic fever (a recurrent, spiking fever). Some physicians, Cardano complained, had gone so far as to recommend consuming gold in order to rejuvenate exhausted powers. Better to do nothing than to do too much, he thought, especially since many medicaments, costly and unpleasant to take, treated symptoms but left the cause of illness unaddressed.

Cardano's criticisms were sincere, but the local medical college was not in a self-critical mood, especially after he also accused its members of hiding their ignorance under a chimera of pride and learning. Paracelsus and Cardano would have agreed on that, albeit for different reasons, but where Cardano offered the medical community (of which he was part) a slap, Paracelsus went for the jugular, harshly critiquing as well the entire occupational group responsible for making the medicines that doctors prescribed: the apothecaries.

So what was Paracelsus reacting against? People had been making medicines since ancient days. Folk medicine and potions made from plants and animals had been part of daily experience in Europe well before Greek medicine organized medical and pharmaceutical thinking, and home-grown traditions continued to supply remedies outside formal, physician-based medicine thereafter. Within official circles, however, Galen supplied the reasoning for why specific medicines worked and for how they should be prepared. Humoral theory provided the guidelines. The pair of qualities associated with each humour (hot–wet, hot–dry, cold–dry, cold–wet) not only defined the type of disease but designated the type of medicine: a hot–wet illness, for example, required ideally a medicine whose qualities were the opposite, in this case cold and dry. Some medicines were called 'simple', since their action followed from one of the qualities. Others were compound medicines, or 'composites', usually a mixture of several substances. These latter packed a double punch, since they delivered more than one quality. This might seem easy, but since every person had his or her own natural balance of humours, and qualities varied by degrees (not everyone became unwell to the same extent), individual remedies needed to be prepared according to a sliding scale. For example, a patient might require a remedy where hot was around a five, and dry about nine. So, not so easy any more.

Galen described 473 drugs made from various substances. Before then, however, the Greek physician Dioscorides (*c.* AD 40–*c.* AD 90) had already expanded the *materia medica* (the substances used in the practice of medicine) of the ancient world during the time of the Roman Empire. Arabic authors would add still more. In the eleventh century one of those authors, a Persian scholar and polymath named Al-Biruni (973–1048), became especially famous for describing medicines whose ingredients came from India and Persia, recording more than a thousand 'simples'. He also recognized pharmacy as a separate branch of the medical arts, a distinction given legal status in the thirteenth century during the reign of the Holy Roman Emperor Friedrich II. According to the legal code called the Constitution of Melfi (1231), academic physicians and apothecaries were of two different walks of life: physicians were scholars and apothecaries were artisans. As artisans, apothecaries needed to follow strictly the recipes that physicians gave them. They also needed to sell their medicines according to an established price and could only open a shop for selling medicines after being granted official approval.

Many Near Eastern medical writings, once discovered and translated into Latin, found their way into Europe in the course of the thirteenth and fourteenth centuries. Many were encyclopaedic in scope and helped provide a broader foundation for Europe's knowledge of making medicinal remedies. The transmission of knowledge, however, is rarely a simple process. In the case of making medicines, confusion abounded concerning what these texts were actually referring to when they described plants and other medicinal substances. Different authors, for instance, used different names for plants. Descriptions of plants with the same name also differed between texts. Medical glossaries attempted to clarify things, but sometimes the ingredients required in a recipe, even when the substances could be identified clearly, were not readily to hand. After all, what grows near Athens or Baghdad may not do well in the soil and climate near Basel. The answer was to create lists of substitutes – in Latin, *quid pro quo* (this for that). For example, since 'mummy' (parts of embalmed corpses from ancient tombs) was hard to get, you could substitute rhubarb.

But it was still easy to make mistakes, and some argued for the need to reform pharmaceutical knowledge completely based more upon local observation than on ancient authority. After reading a recovered text by Dioscorides, the sixteenth-century Italian physician Pietro Andrea Mattioli (1501–1577) became convinced that medical botany in his own time had fallen into a state of utter decay. Plants known in the ancient world could no longer be identified. Mistakes of identification led apothecaries to use the wrong plants, even poisonous ones, in their preparations. Fraud was frequent, and Mattioli hoped that reforming medical botany would produce a more detailed knowledge of 'simples' and allow the errors and frauds of ignorant apothecaries to be more easily recognized.

There might also be more specific rewards once the precise ingredients of ancient recipes came to light. Perhaps one would be able to recreate the aphrodisiac that Paracelsus' namesake, the ancient physician Theophrastus (*c.* 371 – *c.* 287 BC), claimed could produce as many as seventy orgasms. Or perhaps one could make theriac, a complicated medicament described in ancient sources and made up of anywhere from fifty to a hundred ingredients (including, in some recipes, opium and snake flesh), many of them vaguely described or unidentifiable and thus requiring substitutes. This was a drug that could cure everything and was an antidote to every poison. In Naples, the well-known apothecary Ferrante Imperato (*c.* 1525–*c.* 1615) advertised his theriac as being made with only ten substitutes, with later improvements bringing the number down to six.[1]

What Paracelsus advised opened the door to more controversy. He abandoned books of substitutes (the commercial bread and butter of pharmaceutical preparations), prescribed 'little and seldom' and wrote 'short prescriptions', viewing the sort with 'forty to sixty ingredients' with complete disdain – useful, he said, only for bringing more money into the kitchens of apothecaries.[2] As a result, the apothecaries declared him 'strange and eccentric' and, in order to undermine the public's trust, accused him of prescribing and preparing poisons. This was nothing new. Apothecaries and physicians alike often accused one another of the same villainy. After all, the law of the medical marketplace in the Renaissance was, as one medical historian observed, acknowledged to be 'dog-eat-dog'.[3] The 'eccentric' thing here, however, was only Paracelsus' response. Everything in nature, he explained, was a poison unless someone knew how to prepare it properly. To do that, one needed to learn alchemy. Alchemy was, after all, the work of completing nature, and among all the other ways that alchemists did that, the most useful and benevolent was the making of medicines. Making medicines alchemically meant producing them from a wide range of materials that were otherwise poisonous to the body, including minerals and metals, by means of well-known laboratory practices like calcination, sublimation, distillation, coagulation and tincturing. This was alchemy's true bequest to humankind. By failing to understand this, apothecaries had failed their patients, causing them unnecessary suffering and even death. Thus, in the third of his *Seven Defences* Paracelsus censured the procedures and practices of contemporary apothecaries, explaining instead the nature of poisons as part of the process of creation and describing the role of proper alchemical technique – these being necessary for the completion of providence's plan and for the perfection of the body. Underneath his specific response, however, was something so totally beyond the pale as to make both apothecaries and physicians alike stop in their tracks: Galen and Hippocrates, he insisted, had it all wrong in advocating treating illness by means of opposites. Rather, the proper way to treat disease was in accordance with alchemy and nature, and that meant curing like with like.

Nothing in nature was without poison, Paracelsus explained, but by means of alchemy, human artistry separated away what was harmful and impure and delivered to the body what was pure and healthful. Nature and the artisan worked together. Medicine, he observed, was the result of what was made. Human beings, dogs and cats could all eat the same food, but each made a different flesh as a result. In a similar way, nature was available to all, but the alchemist made something different from what anyone else could do. He or she was truly a force of nature, nature's own intelligent agent in making the kind of medicine most efficacious for humankind. By means of laboratory procedures, the alchemist made something beneficial out of things potentially harmful in themselves.

> As it is possible to make something bad from something good, it is also possible to make something good from something bad. [Thus] no one should chastise a thing who does not recognize its transmutation and who does not know what separation does.[4]

Take, for example, the use of arsenic, one of the chief poisons. A drachma can kill a horse. But, 'burn it with *sal nitri* [i.e. potassium nitrate] and it is no longer poison'.[5] The difference is in the preparation, in the action of completing and transmuting nature. The hands of the alchemist were the persistent hands of nature, nature correcting herself for human use in ongoing artistic acts that testified to the fact that the Creation was still in progress.

This, however, was not what nature made when it passed through the hands of traditional apothecaries. Although 'simples' and 'composites' were also produced with the hand – crushing and grinding materials to increase their virtue – what such procedures lacked were the heat-intensive processes of sublimation, calcination and distillation that became the standard procedures of alchemical extraction. These were craft procedures and had, to some degree, already entered Galenic recipe books. Some apothecaries would certainly have known how to make use of them. Others simply did what physicians required. Without alchemical refinement, however, their medicines, Paracelsus argued, had little effect and might become poisons themselves since nothing was taken away from harmful substances. Moreover, without proper attention to dose, everything in nature became hostile to the body and potentially lethal. Probably referring to the treatment for syphilis, he described physicians as anointing patients with quicksilver more thickly than a cobbler anoints leather with grease. They knew how to 'fumigate with its cinnabar' and to 'wash with its sublimate', but, because they lacked alchemical experience, they knew nothing about how to take mercury and separate the good from the bad, the pure from the impure.[6] Imitating nature's mysteries, the alchemist–physician worked where nature left off to perfect further what she had created. University doctors and the apothecaries who served them knew nothing about this. Instead, Paracelsus objects, they did nothing but lead peasants around by the nose, giving them electuaries, syrups, pills and unguents, dispensing nothing but dregs: 'This is how you conduct yourselves in your apothecaries, brewing and rinsing with such great cunning that people conclude that you must be in charge of heaven. In reality, it is the abyss of hell.'[7]

Pharmacy needed an alchemical overhaul, not only because new diseases had overtaken the world since ancient days but because older remedies had been produced on the basis of a false doctrine in regard to treating illness. Making them, in other words, had only made matters worse because these medicines were fashioned as a way to cure disease by means of opposites (for example hot–wet diseases treated by preparations that were cold and dry). The nature of disease, however, as Paracelsus framed it, required something altogether different. As we have seen, he viewed the body as a microcosm reflecting the order and powers of the larger world, with the microcosm and the macrocosm each having its own alchemist. The inner alchemist of the body separated what was useful from what was not, and the external alchemist made medicines to help that separation when the body's alchemical processes got overworked. To know what medicines to make in order to help the inner alchemist do a better job in a specific area, the external alchemist looked to the macrocosm for specific materials designed by God to relate to specific body parts. Nature herself was, in her divine origin, a giant pharmacopoeia in which each part (plants, animals or minerals) was created for the alchemist to treat specific illnesses in the body. The alchemist–physician knew which part of nature to use to treat specific parts of the body because each plant, animal or mineral was 'signed' – we might better say designed – by God for its intended purpose. These were called the signatures of nature, the identifying characteristics of a thing that the attentive physician could use to recognize its intended medicinal use. Plants with certain shapes, colours or tactile qualities, for example, corresponded to the qualities and shapes of specific parts of the body. The alchemist–physician knew how to read the signs and understand the correspondences. Then, selecting the specific part of nature that related to a specific, afflicted part of the body, he or she separated what was pure from what was impure, or even poisonous, by using specific laboratory procedures. Only then did nature's medicine come to light, and it was this that would come to the rescue of an inner alchemist in a specific part of the microcosm.

As disquieting as these ideas were to the learned professionals, the correspondences and signatures described by Paracelsus linking the macrocosm and microcosm were not new ideas at all. Their origins were, in fact, ancient, and the notion had enjoyed a long life in medieval Christian, Jewish and Islamic traditions. A new dimension, however, was added in the fifteenth century. Renaissance scholars, looking for ancient texts of all sorts as a source of pure, uncorrupted knowledge, unearthed writings believed to have been composed by an Egyptian sage and magician – older than Moses, it was claimed – named Hermes Trismegistus (Hermes 'thrice blessed'). Hermes probably never existed (the texts attributed to him turn out to have been written in the early Christian era), but he was very much a reality to Renaissance philosophers. One scholar especially, Marsilio Ficino (1433–1499), was responsible for bringing the texts attributed to Hermes Trismegistus, a collection called the *Corpus Hermeticum*, to light. Through Ficino, Hermetic texts became a major source for esoteric thinking thereafter. These texts described a tradition of knowledge – part theology, part astrology, part magic – in which the natural world was alive with powers. Knowing how to acquire these powers allowed the magus to make use of them to wondrous effect.

Paracelsus was certainly aware of the so-called 'Hermetic tradition' and, as we will see a little later, viewed magic as a feature of the spirit-packed world in which he lived. Finding correspondences in nature was part of that tradition, but Paracelsus added a special twist – not entirely original, but a trademark nevertheless. This was the idea that in defining the relationships between medicines and disease, God had designed local substances which, when properly prepared, would effectively treat local illnesses. The general idea was as old as Hippocrates and had a long folk tradition to support it. Paracelsus, however, made the relationship between indigenous plants and the treatment of homegrown diseases part of his overall medical philosophy. He especially focused on the use of what was local to treat disease in a little bundle of notes composed sometime in the late 1520s, published under the name *Herbarius*.

'Each land', Paracelsus wrote, 'gives birth to its own special kind of sickness, its own medicine, and its own physician', and he could only laugh at those 'who want to prepare medicines from across the seas while there are better remedies to be found in front of their noses'. What grew in their gardens had more advantage than the medical substances imported from exotic places, and if German doctors had more experience in the world, they would recognize 'the deception of merchants, shopkeepers, and sellers of medicines who bring nothing pure to us from foreign shores'. Many substances had become worthless by the time they were delivered to the sick – assuming that it had had any power at all when it was fresh. 'What a terrible thing it is,' Paracelsus complained,

> for someone lying at death's door to gulp down all this merchant's junk with the hope of recovering health . . . It would require a strong enough constitution if

> the stuff were good, let alone if it is counterfeit, spoiled, and really good for nothing.[8]

And what about the books that described medicinal preparations written by German authors for German readers? They contained recipes compiled, for the most part, not by experience but from other books, and in this way resembled the coats of beggars, patched together from all sorts of things. In reality, there was nothing to be found in those books when one needed it most. No one benefited from these writings – except perhaps the printers, who got 'rich and very fat' by publishing them.[9]

For Paracelsus, experience in the fields, mountains, forests and gardens of Germany was a far better teacher than any book, and he used one plant especially as an example of what experience could provide and what traditional humoral medicine had ignored. This was a plant called *Schneerose* or *Schwarze Nieswurz*, known in English as Christmas rose or black hellebore.[10] One could observe that the plant's petals did not wither, even in snow and ice. Rather, they would unfold in the middle of winter and proceed to change colour, first to a reddish-violet and then to green, becoming leaves that nourished the plant in the next year. For the physician with eyes to see, these were all signs designating its medicinal purpose. The plant was communicating through signs that among its hidden powers were preservative virtues. Paracelsus took note and described an elixir for long life made from its dried leaves. Medicines prepared from the plant's root, he said, cured epilepsy, podagra (gout), stroke and dropsy. It also guarded against infections, promoted menstruation and the expulsion of difficult miscarriages that could not be removed in any other way. This was a plant known since ancient times. 'The most ancient of the first philosophers', Paracelsus noted, 'employed the plant as a medicine [for patients] after reaching the age of sixty and continuing its use until the end of their lives.' They thus 'came away without sickness and reached the end of their lives with sound body. In them were found no ulcers or abscesses, neither in the lungs, liver, spleen or anywhere else.' But then, he laments, arose the 'humor doctors', and these 'attended to their own unfounded theory, without knowledge of the genuine properties of nature'. As a result, 'the bottom fell out of medicine', and knowledge of the plant 'was struck from the mind altogether'.[11]

In the Renaissance most medicines were still made from plants. However, Paracelsus and later Paracelsian physicians came to prefer mineral remedies, since these related best to the active beginnings of all things – Sulphur, Salt and Mercury – which defined as well three arenas of disease: namely, sulphurous, saline and mercurial. To prepare medicines from these substances, the alchemist–physician needed to use the techniques of distilling and sublimating, using heat to separate the more volatile parts of a body from the rest and then condensing the subtilized portion through cooling into a concentrated form, either a liquid (distillation) or a solid (sublimation). These procedures had been around for a long time, having been introduced to Europe, along with a number of assaying practices, by way of translated Arabic texts. Distillation procedures especially had become part of the common repertoire of many herbalists, allowing them to produce a variety of distilled waters from plants. Something new, however, occurred in the thirteenth and fourteenth centuries, a new alchemical way of preparing medicines that greatly influenced Paracelsus' techniques and which fitted precisely within the contours of his medical cosmology. It began with the distillation of wine.

When the volatile parts of wine were driven off and then condensed, the resulting product displayed astonishing properties. It was a water that could burn, an *aqua ardens*. It preserved vegetable and animal matter, postponing decay. And it could dissolve substances (including resins and oils) that could not be dissolved in water. Its name, derived from an Arabic root, was alcohol. Using alcohol and other dissolving agents, alchemists were able to extract the subtle, more volatile and sometimes aromatic parts of a substance. In doing so, many believed that they were extracting something spiritual and celestial, a heavenly, perfecting substance that gave being and activity to each created thing and accounted for life itself. Extractions of this sort were given new names, sometimes called an elixir of life (*elixir vitae*), sometimes designated as a *quinta essentia* or fifth essence.

Among those who wrote about the powers of the *quinta essentia* was a French Franciscan friar named Jean de Roquetaillade (John of Rupescissa, *c.* 1310–1366/70). Based on his own apocalyptic visions, Rupescissa thought that a clash with the armies of the Antichrist was fast approaching. In that battle, the old social order would be overturned and those who followed Christ would be aided in their fight against the minions of the Antichrist by a special form of knowledge derived from the study of the natural world, the knowledge of alchemy. This knowledge would, he believed, replenish the economic and physical vigour of the righteous. It could restore and prolong their health. The gold needed to sustain the effort to bring about a better world could be concealed through amalgamation. Soldiers could carry jars of *aqua ardens* (alcohol) to treat their wounds. In spreading the word of God and reshaping society, itinerant preachers could prepare a salve to heal their sore feet. Rupescissa explained that his alchemical insights had come to him through revelation, not practical experience, although he does seem to have had a good knowledge of alchemical procedures. Regardless, he was able to explain how medicines could be made by extracting an essence that was celestial in origin (their *quinta essentia*) from terrestrial substances.[12] This fifth essence, and the way to make medicinal tinctures by means of it, became the focus of a book written while Rupescissa languished for a while in a French prison (the Pope was not happy with his prophecies). His ideas, however, inspired others. They were soon taken up by another Franciscan, named Roger Bacon, and served to underscore the writings of two of the best known alchemical writers of the later Middle Ages, Arnold of Vilanova and Ramon Lull, both often confused with figures of the same name.

Like Rupescissa, the alchemist Arnold (to distinguish him from the Catalan physician and religious reformer also called Arnold of Villanova, *c.* 1240–1311) linked alchemy with Christian theology, believing that a philosophers' stone capable of 'healing' metals and bringing them to perfection could be obtained by means of a preparation of mercury. According to the alchemist Lull (to distinguish him from the philosopher and logician, also Spanish, of the same name who died in 1315), physical creation began when God brought into being *argent vive* – what we call quicksilver or mercury. This, for Lull, was the original matter of everything else. At its most subtle, it made up the bodies of angels; in the physical universe, it composed the fifth essence of heavenly spheres. When it came to the formation of earthly things, a coarser *argent vive* made the elements – earth, air, fire and water – and yet in every terrestrial thing, there also remained a part of the heavenly stuff, the fifth essence, and it was by means of this essence that the heavens influenced growth and decay, generation and corruption, in earthly beings. All things, even things apparently inert, possessed a kind of life because they were connected to this life-giving source of being. The task of the Lullian alchemist was to find ways to extract this fifth essence and increase its power. *Aqua ardens* (alcohol) was the link. Viewed as the quintessence of wine, alcohol (refined through multiple distillations) became the means of dissolving herbs and other materials and extracting their celestial parts.[13]

Medical alchemy, like the hermetic cosmology of signatures and correspondences, anticipated Paracelsus' theoretical and practical innovations, and influences of a different sort – especially about distillation practices and working with metals – resulted from his personal experience in the practices of mining. Paracelsus, in other words, did not work in a vacuum. He benefited from the experiences of others, and books of various practical sorts were available for him to read. Preceding traditions of making and explaining impacted his own beliefs and procedures, and he readily acknowledged their influence. In one text, his *Grossen Wundarznei* (Great Surgery), written around 1536, he observed that since childhood he had been instructed in the *adepta philosophia* (that is, alchemy), as

well as in ancient and modern writings – by his father and other teachers, notably bishops and abbots. His father had also introduced him to men well trained in smelting and assaying, who therefore had great experience in mining and metallurgy. Many of their practices had never been recorded. Nevertheless, several German handbooks related to mining and metallurgy came into print during Paracelsus' early years, and he probably knew of these as well. One was called a *Well Ordered and Useful Little Book about How to Seek and Find Mines*. It appeared in 1505, written by a physician in Freiberg named Ulrich Rülein von Calw (*c*. 1465–1523). Later in Paracelsus' lifetime the well-known German humanist Georgius Agricola (1494–1555) published, in the form of a dialogue, a treatise on metallurgy called *Bermannus* (1530), a prequel to his much more famous treatise on mining and metallurgy, *De re metallica* (On the Nature

9 Distillation, from Hieronymus Brunschwig, *Liber de arte distillandi* (Book on the Art of Distillation, *c*. 1500).

of Metals, 1556). Other books that Paracelsus may have known described mining operations, and the preparations of acids and salts that were part of assaying techniques. One was called *Nützliches Bergbüchlein* (A Useful Little Book of Mining); another was simply titled *Probierbüchlein* (A Little Book Concerning Assaying). The latter especially was reprinted frequently, often emended with new material, and Paracelsus would have found a handy reference in any one of them.

Practices of distillation were also well represented in book form, and such volumes would have been ready to hand at the monasteries and cloisters that Paracelsus tells us were the sites of his early education. A little book concerning distilled waters, *Büchlein von den Ausgebrannten Wässern*, attributed to the Viennese physician Michael Puff (also called Michael Schrick), described plant distillates in 83 chapters and saw over twenty printings between 1477 and 1500. Also frequently reprinted were the books on distillation by the Strasbourg surgeon Hieronymus Brunschwig (*c.* 1450–*c.* 1512). Brunschwig's *Kleines Destillierbuch* (Little Book of Distillation), published in 1500, described various distillation vessels and methods as well as a list of medicinal products related to illnesses arranged 'from head to foot'. This was followed twelve years later by a larger text, *Grosse Destillierbuch* (Big Book of Distillation), which added entries on alchemical preparations and the *quinta essentia*, and also contained a *thesaurus pauperum*, a medical formulary of cheap medicines for the poor (illus. 9, 10).

Sometimes books were merged together for the purposes of reprinting them as anthologized volumes. The German physician Eucharius Rösslin (the younger) joined Brunschwig's *Kleines Destillierbuch* to an early German herbal of 1485 called

Gart der Gesundheit (Garden of Health), thus creating a new book, called *Kräuterbuch von Allem Erdgewächs* (Herbal of All Growing Things), that was published four times in the 1530s and three times in the decade following. With just a little facility in Latin, one could also read Philipp Ulstadt's *Coelum philosophorum, seu, De secretis naturae liber* (The Heavens of the Philosophers; or, A Book Concerning the Secrets of Nature), which appeared on bookshelves around 1528, much of it concerned with distillations of alcohol (that is, spirit of wine).

It is hard to judge how many remedies Paracelsus knew about, developed or actually used. Sometimes only a name remains, but there are about seven hundred recipes that can still be studied. Of these, approximately 250 recipes contain chemical (including metallic and mineral) ingredients. Only a handful (about 7 per cent) follow entirely from the alchemical methods that he described.[14] Despite his criticisms of contemporary doctors, humoral theory and medical practice, he did not reject completely the remedies described by Dioscorides, Galen and other ancient physicians. Some of these had, after all, established themselves with a long and successful track record, and Paracelsus knew not to throw the baby out with the bathwater. Nevertheless, some things that were old got new treatments. Opium, for instance (used in ancient Greece as a medicine and, in combination with hemlock, for a painless suicide), could be dissolved in alcohol and prepared into a tincture. Paracelsus called it 'laudanum', from a Latin verb meaning 'to praise', and sought to increase its potency and utility by preparing it with other ingredients, including crushed pearls, amber and musk.

Influences and precursors aside, Paracelsus certainly knew his way around the laboratory, and, in a famous letter, one of his assistants, Johannes Oporinus (1507–1568), who later became a printer in Basel, described him at work in his *officina carbonaria*, his alchemical workshop. There we find him making sublimated oils, including an oil of arsenic – *crocus martis*, usually a strong metallic purgative – and what was most likely a liniment called 'Oppodeldoch'.[15] Like other alchemical spaces, Paracelsus' *officina* would have been equipped with ovens and furnaces as well as the vessels and instruments well known to metallurgists, gold- and silversmiths, distillers, potters, glassmakers and artists. Crucibles, retorts, vials, flasks, alembics and pelicans were part of the furniture of such alchemical sites,

10 A distilling oven, from Hieronymus Brunschwig, *Liber de arte distillandi* (Book on the Art of Distillation, *c.* 1500).

and Paracelsus refers to them and to their uses when describing laboratory practices of resolving, dissolving, distilling, subliming, extracting, calcining and coagulating.

Most of the materials he used had also been around for a long time, and some had made their way into the established *materia medica*. Notably, he worked with mercury and recommended mercury preparations as a diuretic and for treating syphilis and dropsy. He also worked with gold and regarded preparations of gold – such as *aurum potabile* (drinkable gold), quintessence of gold, magisterium of gold and the tincture of gold – as supreme perfecting agents and panaceas. Most important in his recipes were the sulphides of lead, copper and mercury, and Paracelsus made special use of one of these, the sulphide mineral antimony, to create several remedies, including oil of antimony, tincture of antimony and flowers of antimony. Depending upon its preparation, antimony could be used for different purposes. Red antinomy made into an oil treated leprosy. The same oil, produced by a different process, treated wounds.

Other parts of the alchemical pharmacy – including metallic oxides (lead, iron, copper, zinc), verdigris (copper acetate), alum, white lead (lead carbonate) and various vitriols (acids) – were also part of the material inventory with which artisans of various sorts worked every day. To learn about them, however, required the physician to leave home, to consult with people who experienced the materials and forces of nature through the use of their hands. University physicians were rank amateurs in this regard. 'All you ever do is read,' Paracelsus admonished them, 'Here it says this. There it says that . . . If no one had written it you wouldn't know a thing.'[16]

The most effective way to learn how the world was made was from people who made things. Only then could one test the writings of authorities and assay their truth. Writings that came about in this way would survive, Paracelsus predicted. The other sort, the stuff of the universities, would be torn asunder and acknowledged as 'replete with gall, poison, and the viper's brood and will be hated by people as they hate toads'.[17] The true physician needed to get into the world. He or she needed to travel.

FOUR

Pursuing the Arts Where God Has Placed Them: On the Road for the Sake of Learning

In the second half of the twelfth century, a versifier known only as the 'Arch poet' wrote the lines: 'My aim is to perish in a tavern/ So that the wine will be close to my dying mouth/ Then choirs of angels will sing merrily/ "May God be merciful to this drunk".' The poem, titled 'His Confession', is famous for professing a love of women, gambling and drinking, and elsewhere the same poet offers an intimate portrait of a wandering, vagabond life. The two went together – being drunk and being a wanderer – and Paracelsus was denounced and condemned for being both. What this meant is that he kept, and enjoyed, the company of students, beggars, itinerant artisans and wayfarers, the marginal folk of towns and villages. He travelled and thought travelling essential to learning. Being often on the road, Paracelsus' regular companions were people who knew how to survive there. If he got drunk, as his enemies claimed he often did, it was probably with these students, beggars, travelling scholars and with those who worked with their hands, those who were poor. He spoke their languages, the neo-Latin of travelling scholars and students (the language of the Arch poet), the colloquial German of tradesmen and artisans, and the private jargon of beggars and vagabonds. His secretary for three years, Johannes Oporinus, wrote spitefully in a letter that Paracelsus was hardly ever sober and that, later in his life, he drank peasants under the table in drinking contests. He was also drunk when he dictated his medical philosophy, says Oporinus, but he admits that the results were so lucid that someone who was completely temperate could not have done better.[1]

He was, Paracelsus said of himself, a resident of nowhere; and in the fourth of his *Seven Defences*, he responded to those who considered him to be less worthy as a physician because of his journeying and lack of a fixed place. What he did, he explained, was for the common man, and it was for common people that he sought out the arts where they were to be found. This could not be done by staying at home in some cosy chimney corner but required that he pursue the arts where they were to be found, spread out over the whole world. 'If someone wants to recognize many diseases, well, then, he has to travel; if he travels far, he'll experience a lot, and will come to know just as much.'[2] This was certainly better than sitting at home by the stove. Only 'the cushion sitters' had a problem with journeying, the very people who couldn't get to the shoemaker's for a pair of shoes on their own. The arts could not be 'held in vats' or 'nailed up in a barrel'.[3] The mountains do not come to us, after all; nor do the artisans who make preparations from nature just appear at our door. The physician–alchemist has to find the *mineralia* where they exist in nature and has to call upon those who know how to grasp nature and make useful things. This is how one learnt to separate the pure from the dross, by gauging the real experience of the hand.

Searching out what worked was an obligation for the physician, so why did his opponents despise and spit on the person who did it? Maybe Paracelsus' accusers were afraid of the highway; after all, they might be killed or robbed. He was not worried, however. He had nothing, so had nothing to lose. He could roam happily. 'Whoever wants to search through [nature],' he instructed,

> must tread her books with [his] feet. Scripture is fathomed by means of its letters; but nature by means of [wandering from] land to land. As many lands as there are, there are just as many pages. Thus is the book of nature; thus must one turn her pages.[4]

Stay-at-home physicians had no knowledge of this book, and if it were not for those who gained experience by travelling, the slaughter of patients at their hands would be all the greater. However, when they realized how much was to be gained through such experience, those same physicians would 'send off their rats to travel'.[5]

Truly, Paracelsus was hardly ever at rest. But the extent of his travels is not at all clear, at least not in the early years. The real question is how much credit should be given to what he says about his own wanderings. If we are to believe what he says, the story is as follows. After spending a long time studying in German, Italian and French schools in search of the foundations of medicine, he began to wander, seeking out those experienced in the art – not learned physicians, but barbers, bathers, women, necromancers, alchemists, those living in cloisters; he consulted the noble as well as commoners, the intelligent as well as the simple minded. The pursuit took him through Italy to Spain, England, Scandinavia, Portugal, the Netherlands, Central and Eastern Europe, Turkey and the Middle East. Much of this may have been boasting or a literary means of self-fashioning, a way of constructing an identity emphatically different from the professional norm. Even so, we do know that Paracelsus spent part of his early life as a military surgeon, and there were plenty of wars to keep him busy in any of a number of places. With no documentary evidence to support his claims, scholars of Paracelsus are suspicious of many of his personal reflections. His residence in Scandinavia as surgeon in the army of Christian II seems to be pure fantasy; and what credence can be allotted to the effect of a wound potion capable of curing everything except fractures and vascular injuries when he claims to have witnessed its use at 'Stockholm in Denmark?' Surviving letters and other documents lend more credibility to the details of his movements upon leaving Basel in 1528. These have a far more local feel, often focusing on localities in southern Germany, Alsace, Switzerland, Austria and Bohemia.

And yet Paracelsus is betwixt and between these places as well, staying for various lengths of time in cities like Salzburg, Strasbourg, Basel, Nuremberg, Augsburg, Ulm, Innsbruck, Pressburg (now Bratislava) and Vienna; and visiting smaller places and regions like Colmar, Esslingen, St Gallen, Memmingen, Beratzhausen, the mining districts of Appenzell and Sterzing, as well as locales famous for their medicinal waters,

St Moritz and Pfäfers.[6] In many places, he met resistance from local medical communities and apothecaries. Others praised him. Oporinus, for all his invective, noted that following his departure from Basel, Paracelsus was, in the region of Alsace, celebrated as a second Asclepius among rustics and those more refined.[7] His knowledge of the Bible let him combine preaching with healing (on which more later), and among peasants, he must have stood out not just as a second Asclepius but as a lay practitioner of souls, a poor man's custodian of scripture and salvation. He was a traveller, a spiritual vagabond and medical vagrant; but he always kept company with Christ. After all, Jesus travelled, was a healer and apparently didn't mind a glass of wine.

That sort of comparison would have been lost, however, on those sanctioned with official religious and social authority. As the sociologist and cultural anthropologist Roland Girtler explains, their reputation for tricks and deceit meant travelling people were kept at arm's length by the major reformers.[8] For Calvin, for example, their occupations were in no way pleasing to God. Luther went further, publicly condemning wanderers and beggars, and writing the introduction to the 1528 edition of one of the most important texts alerting readers to the tricks, deceptions and language of different sorts of vagrants and petty crooks, the so-called *Liber vagatorum* (Book of Wanderers, first published around 1500). He had good reason to intervene, having himself, he admitted, once fallen victim to their treachery: 'I myself this past year was cheated and led astray more than I want to admit by such tramps and pettifoggers.' The purpose of the book, Luther proclaimed, was that everyone – especially princes, lords and city councillors – might get smart to the ways of beggars and vagrants, and so that every city and village could distinguish its own deserving poor from the myriad undeserving paupers: fake pilgrims, repentant executioners and prostitutes, released prisoners and women pretending to be pregnant or insane (the latter letting themselves be led around in chains). The book also provided a mini-dictionary of *Rotwelsch*,[9] the jargon of vagabonds and beggars.[10] Luther identified the language as having Jewish roots, 'as those well know who understand Hebrew'. He was partly right. The word for *Gott* (God), for example, was *Adone*, from the Hebrew *Adonai*. Yet, other words had different origins. A pretty virgin (*hübsche Jungfrau*) was 'Wunnenberg', after a town (Bad Wünnenberg), presumably one with lots of pretty girls. The language of the beggar (*Breger*) was really a mixture of languages, including Latin and vernacular Romance dialects, some parts of which were already in use three centuries before.

Paracelsus knew this language, and he did not have to look words up in mini-dictionaries to understand it. He lived it, on the road and in the tavern, crossing borders both socially and intellectually, in possession of his own free spirit. According to Oporinus, although Paracelsus liked to dress well and had new clothes made every month, once he put them on, he never changed out of them. He was sometimes mistaken for a wagoner, and on one occasion, so the story goes, the city of Innsbruck refused him entry on account of his run-down appearance. What a sight he must have been when his clothes got so soiled that, as Oporinus also writes, they were hard to give away.[11] Regardless, he knew and cared for the poor, and when he died – after his feudal lord, the abbot got his cut

– Paracelsus left everything remaining of his wardrobe and personal effects to the suffering and poor of Salzburg.

By travelling, Paracelsus not only observed new regions and new diseases. He observed how people lived. In treating illness, he argued, the physician had to know how to be artful, and it is quite clear that in thinking about how a physician learnt his or her art, Paracelsus was thinking about how anyone learnt a trade. Any sort of tradesman, he explained, had to be trained in that vocation since childhood. What applied to the crafts and trades in the way of lifelong experience applied all the more to medicine, because medicine was an art that required more learning than all the rest. Experience in medicine meant knowing what was useful in every circumstance. Knowing what was useful in the natural world required looking carefully at plants, animals and minerals and recognizing their signatures, correspondences and hidden virtues. Furthermore, to be truly artful, the experienced physician had to know how people spent their lives and how their routines affected their health. Since the trades required lifelong immersion in environments, materials and tasks, the physician had to know what was useful to those who pursued specific occupations – 'to the fisherman, to the leather worker, to the tanner, to the dyer, to the smith of metals', as well as knowing 'what is the business of a traveller and what of someone who is stationary'?[12]

Physicians had to be taught about mineral diseases in places where those afflicted by them actually lived. Physicians needed to visit the mines. Travelling to the Tyrolean Alps in the mid-1520s, Paracelsus came to know what was useful to miners. He had grown up in their company and knew how to talk to them. Many suffered from diseases of the lungs and from the afflictions caused by poisonous metals and fumes, but there was nothing written about such diseases in ancient texts. The book that he subsequently wrote, titled *Von der Bergsucht oder Bergkranckheiten drey Bücher* (Concerning Miners' Consumption; or, Three Books of Mining Illnesses), appeared in the 1530s, but the original text is lost and the writing that remains appeared in the later 1560s, long after Paracelsus' death. Despite this textual lacuna, many scholars believe that the later treatise genuinely is Paracelsus' earlier work. Unlike other works on mining published at the time, Paracelsus' text is not at all concerned with mining technology. Rather, it is a medical document that is concerned, above all, with diseases related to mining and connected activities like smelting and assaying, and as such, it is regarded as one of the very earliest medical monographs specifically concerned with industrial or occupational illness.

The book was part of a larger plan to bring physicians more in touch with the lives of people who worked with their hands. Social reform was always on Paracelsus' mind, and he thought that physicians had a role to play in altering the circumstances and treating the ills of those who struggled daily with back-breaking work. But these were dangerous times. In the 1520s peasants in Germany were in revolt, seeking redress for social and economic abuse and disadvantage. Luther turned against them. They were no better than highwaymen and murderers, he proclaimed, deserving death in body and soul. Clearly those who lived their lives upon the highway threatened both secular authority and the stability of the social order; indeed, the highway itself could well be imagined on religious and social grounds to be an avenue of blasphemy and rebellion.

Despite the dangers from beggars and vagabonds, tradespeople were nevertheless often on the road. Merchants travelled constantly, visiting trade fairs and seeking customers. Later in the century a merchant from Nuremberg named Balthasar Paumgartner (1551–1600) had been travelling so much on business that he had lost a great deal of weight and was thoroughly exhausted. He also had more specific complaints, digestive issues and a nagging headache; it was time to visit a bath. He visited four of them between 1584 and 1596 and wrote about the cures at each in letters to his wife back home, Magdalena. One time he stayed for only eight days. On another occasion, he stayed for three months. His doctors thought that his liver was the problem: it needed refreshing. So he drank the waters (two and a half litres a day for three days was prescribed) and took purgatives to clean him out. He bathed for hours and took head showers. He developed an itch; he bathed some more. To beat back the boredom, he turned to alcohol when he could, took walks (sweating was good for you) and became a spectator of those who gambled for high stakes (he claimed to his wife never to have taken part). Sometimes he felt better, but never for long, and at the end of the fourth visit, he still complained of being constantly tormented by stomach pains and rheumatic inflammations. What to do? Although the correspondence breaks off here, Balthasar may well have returned for another round of bathing soon thereafter. Baths, after all, were popular and a way for those troubled by aches and pains to do something about them, trying new waters and new regimens, sometimes close to home, sometimes travelling to fashionable baths far away.[13]

Travelling to bathing locations and taking the waters in specific places had been a part of medical culture since the Middle Ages. The most reputed baths were in Italy, and over the course of the thirteenth and fourteenth centuries an entire literature about bathing appeared there. One author, Pietro d'Abano (1257–*c.* 1315), noted different types of bath, distinguishing between the sweating bath, the air bath, the shower, the herb bath, the herb steam bath and the natural bath. In a natural bath, the water was warmed naturally – he thought, by a warming sulphur. The waters of a bath-house, on the other hand, were artificially heated. Other writers emphasized the relation between specific minerals and healing qualities for specific parts of the body. Natural waters containing alum helped treat parts affected by apoplexy. Waters containing bitumen purged poisonous matter. For those seeking baths with specific minerals, Pietro's student Gentile da Foligno (d. 1348) provided a list. Some were excellent sources of saltpetre, while others were notable for containing copper, iron, alum or sulphur. All counteracted the effect of excessively wet and cold qualities among the humours (illus. 11).[14]

Natural springs and bathing rooms often existed together, and some guides offered visitors assistance by instructing them about accommodations and regimens. Visitors themselves wrote reviews of baths recording descriptions, experiences and analyses of the waters and, significantly, documenting their opinions. Some expressed concern about when and when not to use certain waters. Another form of writing expressed

11 A bathing scene, from Conrad Gesner, *Corpus venetum de balneis* (1553).

a different sort of concern related to the use of baths, one more moral than medical. A good example is a letter of 1416 by the Italian writer Poggio Bracciolini. Poggio was worried about so many people, young and old, cleric and lay, and of opposite sexes, getting (more or less) naked together (illus. 12). Surely, the temptation was to have sex; and was this not the reason why so many people went to the baths in the first place? A similar view, with an added twist, became part of one of the earliest guides to bathing, written by a German author named Felix Hemmerli.[15]

Hemmerli was trained in law, not medicine, and in a text that he composed around 1450, he not only described specific German baths but held physicians accountable for having kept information about them secret. Without medical direction, many people, rather than going to the baths for

12 The immorality of the baths, in Hans Bock the Elder, *The Baths at Leuk*, 1597, oil painting.

therapeutic reasons, had, he thought, only made use of them for the purpose of satisfying their sexual desires.[16] Hemmerli's treatise may have been an overreaction, but it did inspire physicians to create their own, more medically oriented literature. On the one hand, this literature helped to guide visitors needing to know about the comfort of structures and how to procure provisions (Balthasar Paumgartner found a man at one bath who sold him a rabbit and several chickens). On the other hand, the new medical literature went further, directly addressing the person who was struggling with an illness and who wanted to know what baths in specific regions had to offer, and what illnesses were best treated by which specific regimens of bathing, showering and drinking waters.

One of these books, one of the most popular in the German language, was written by the physician, astrologer and geographer Lorenz Fries (*c.* 1490–*c.* 1532), who, at least for a time, was a good friend of Paracelsus. It was called *Traktat der Wildbäder Natur, Wirkung, und Eigenschaft* (Treatise on the Nature, Effects and Properties of Natural Baths, 1519) and it is probably what inspired Paracelsus to write his own short text in the mid- to late 1520s in which he recommends bathing and discusses the effect of certain waters upon specific illnesses.[17] He also recommended the waters of specific baths, among them the baths at Pfäfers, Baden im Aargau, Baden-Baden, Wildbad and Liebenzell, as well as a number of thermal baths, especially the baths at Teplitz in Bohemia (now Teplice, Czech Republic), Plombières, Gastein and one near St Gallen. Of them all, it was Bad Pfäfers in the Oberschweiz that most held his attention. This was a popular place and could boast prominent guests. One was an imperial knight

– who was also a poet, satirist and religious reformer – named Ulrich von Hutten (1488–1523). He visited the baths in the early 1520s, followed its regimens, but left with the complaints he came with.

Paracelsus was not a bathing practitioner, but he did write about them, and by doing so once again consorted with people whom society considered to be disreputable. Most bathers

13 Bathers and cuppers in an illustration by Jost Amman for Hans Sachs's *Ständebuch* (Book of Trades, 1568).

were also barbers. They offered sweating and tub baths, they cut hair, shaved, bled, massaged and, on occasion, treated wounds (illus. 13). But that was not all, and as early descriptions make clear, the baths could also be centres of indulgence and sexual promiscuity. Bathers and their attendants knew how to arrange things. Debaucheries and drunken dinners were part of the scene – and if this was not in reality evident everywhere, it was still very much the public perception. And yet it would be inaccurate to insist that this was the whole story. While critical of some bathers and barbers who also advertised themselves as wound physicians (more on this practice shortly) – and who were motivated primarily by greed – Paracelsus' circle of friends included bathers who were of long standing in their communities and who were generally thought of as honourable and respectable citizens. Of all the baths in and around Salzburg, perhaps the best known and most successful was the Rappelbad. The family Rappel had managed it for two hundred years, and Paracelsus was good friends with Hans and Wolfgang Rappel, the present owner-operators. Another master barber, Andrä Wendel, established himself as an esteemed wound physician, becoming a citizen of Salzburg in 1534. His was a firm friendship with Paracelsus, so much so that he inherited, upon his friend's death, all of Paracelsus' medical books and everything that pertained to making his medicines.[18]

The medical marketplace with which Paracelsus involved himself was made up of prestigious university doctors who administered mostly to a wealthy clientele and who sometimes held posts as city or court physicians. As city physicians,

they communicated with the wider urban population, mostly in writing, composing self-help books and explaining recipes for those enduring the most common complaints. There were also approved healers – including apothecaries and midwives – and a special group of artisanal, hands-on practitioners called wound physicians. In terms of numbers and varieties of cases, and in attending to specific problems in need of correction through surgical means, the wound physicians did the heavy lifting (illus. 14). Sometimes wound physicians were also barbers or bathers, and although local guilds tried to protect surgical healers by limiting the number of practitioners, there always remained competition with other healers. Jost Amman and Hans Sachs, in their *Book of Trades* (1568), give us a picture of the practical day-to-day work of a barber who was also a wound physician:

14 Wound physicians at work in an engraving by Jost Amman, *c.* 1565.

> I am called everywhere/ can make healthy salves/ fresh wounds I can heal with grace/ the same with broken legs and old injuries/ I can cure the French disease/ couch for cataracts/ treat burns and pull teeth/ I can also barber/ shave and trim/ Also I happily let blood.[19]

Bathers and barbers separated company in the late Renaissance, for both economic and material reasons. A lack of bathing houses may have prevented some assistants from setting up their own concessions, and, oddly, the use of soap for shaving – replacing the uncomfortable dry shave – has been suggested as a reason for people beginning to take care of their own personal appearance. Whatever the motive, it was barbers rather than bathers who began to take over the practice of bleeding and cupping, and also, since the knife was close at hand, of treating and suturing small wounds. Some understood more complicated surgical techniques and became well-respected practitioners. These often set themselves up as wound physicians, as was the case with Paracelsus' friend Andrä Wendel. One recent study estimates that, depending on the size of the practitioner's town or city, the practices of these surgeons might cater to hundreds, perhaps thousands of people. What this tells us is that, despite attempts to stigmatize them as employing disreputable manual practices connected with blood and broken bodies, wound physicians often treated a variety of complaints and maintained good relations with urban elites, and some even rose to the social status of citizens, paying taxes and contracting marriages with families of the merchant middle class.

Nevertheless, a pressing visit to a wound physician was usually an act of desperation, and patients knew what they were in for. Later in the century – in a text that boasted of describing all the professions of the world, *La piazza universale di tutte le professioni del mondo* (The Universal Piazza of all the Professions of the World, 1585) – the eclectic Italian writer Tommaso Garzoni (1549–1589) noted that wound physicians cut away what was joined to the human body and joined again what had been cut off, hindering without pain all putrefaction and decay. These physicians, he continues, worked by means of cautery, stitching, separating, cutting, burning and letting blood. They also eliminated, cleansed and grafted flesh, and wrapped, applied and tied bandages to prevent air from getting to wounds. They also, of course, used tools: among the most important were knives, saws, needles, files, rasps, splints (with and without screws), spatulas, plasters, bandages and pincers – lots of pincers, large and small, sharp and smooth, rounded and pointed.[20] With these instruments, and others, wound physicians began to specialize. While nearly all could use cautery to stop bleeding or to treat abscesses, skin tumours and haemorrhoids, others, more daring, stitched up hernias, sutured anal fissures or cut for bladder stones. In Italy one famous surgeon, Gaspare Tagliacozzi (1545–1599), developed a technique to graft skin from the forearm to rebuild noses mutilated in sword fights or in accidents.

Surgical techniques were also being developed on the battlefield, especially with the introduction of gunpowder into warfare. As he reports in his own account of the event, the French surgeon Ambroise Paré (*c.* 1510–1590) was asked if anything could be done for two soldiers horribly disfigured by gunpowder. He said nothing could; the burns were too severe to be treated. An old soldier thereupon put the soldiers out of their misery, cutting their throats, 'gently, and without ill will toward them', telling Paré that if he were in the same condition he would pray to God that someone would do the same for him.[21] Paré's first book was called *Methode de traicter les playes faictes par hacquebutes et aultres bastons à feu* (The Method of Curing Wounds Caused by Arquebus and Firearms, 1545), published just a few years after Paracelsus' death. It was followed nearly two decades later by Paré's *Treatise on Surgery*, just as many of Paracelsus' books began to appear in print. Both of Paré's texts were seminal works that described new surgical techniques for treating battlefield wounds. For instance, rather than treating gunshot wounds with boiling elderberry oil and cauterization, he created his own recipe to keep infection at bay, using egg yolk, oil of roses and turpentine.[22] He advocated amputation, rather than cautery, operating through healthy tissues and attempting to form vascular ligatures, tying off blood vessels to arrest haemorrhage.

Paracelsus, of course, was no longer alive when Paré's books were published, but much of what Paré put in writing about surgical practice was 'in the air', and Paracelsus probably knew of two other surgical texts greatly influenced by their author's experience on the battlefield. The first, called the *Buch der Wundartzney* (Book of Surgery), was published in 1497 by Hieronymus Brunschwig, whom we met earlier in connection with his book of distillation and who was the author of one of the first surgical books to illustrate surgical instruments. The other book of battlefield medicine was the *Feldtbuch der Wundarztnei* (Fieldbook of Surgery, 1517) by Hans von Gersdorff

(1455–1529), a book that, along with representing numerous surgical instruments, illustrated techniques for treating specific battlefield injuries (illus. 15). Paracelsus evidently had a special connection to this volume, since many of the illustrations in it appeared again in the 1536 edition of one of his

15 Battlefield wound surgery, from Hans von Gersdorff, *Feldtbuch der Wundartzney* (1530).

Der Ander Theyl

Der grossen Wundartzeney deß weitberhümpten/ bewerten/ vnnd erfarnen/ Theophrasti Paracelsi von Hohenheym/ der Leib vnd Wundartzney Doctorn/ Von der offnen Schäden vrsprung vnd heylung. Auß rechtem grundt vnnd bewerten stücken treuwlich an Tag geben.

Mit Röm. Keys. Maiestet Freyheit nicht nach zudrucken.

16 Title page of Paracelsus' *Der Grossen Wundartzney* (The Great Surgery, 1536).

own most important writings – and one of the few that appeared during his lifetime – *Der Grossen Wundartzney* (The Great Surgery) (illus. 16).

For doctors who were not also surgeons Paracelsus had nothing but scorn, and at the beginning of his *Great Surgery* he added a letter from an Augsburg doctor named Wolfgang Thalhauser, who, like Paracelsus, claimed to be both a regular physician and wound doctor, or surgeon. Thalhauser was blunt: 'At one time,' he wrote,

> the Romans, for much less reason, threw out all their physicians from the city. If the same authorities were alive now, I dare say they might not suffer any of today's physicians in the whole empire, for there is no art, no understanding, no order in medicine any longer.[23]

Thalhauser regarded university doctors to be the chief cause of 'this corruption and inhuman injury'.[24] After all, a good physician needed to know three things: namely, the body, illnesses and the medicines or therapies with which to treat them. If the physician's lack of surgical knowledge was one problem, Thalhauser also recognized another. Because so many people turned to wound physicians to treat their problems, many of the latter had become greedy – more interested in making money with their limited knowledge than in truly understanding the art of healing the sick. Previously, shavers, bathers, cuppers and barbers had functioned as servants and attendants to doctors. Now, however, they had become 'bad money doctors', so common and cheap that it was not at all surprising that 'the art itself has become costly and strange'.[25]

No one travelled anymore seeking the art. A couple of hundred recipes either copied out of books or inherited in some other way set one up as a healer, and a reputation could be made not because of one's own knowledge and success, but because of another's failure. If there was an injury that required a surgeon, Thalhauser continues, a physician was suddenly out of his realm:

> There comes then a barber or bather who knows nothing of human complexions. He might as well be a butcher and the patient a pig. He simply cuts, burns, patches up, and pulls apart at his own pleasure, and no one can object to why he does it, for the university doctor has not learned about, nor has ever seen [the things he confronts].[26]

No wonder the art was in a shambles. Surgical practices were entirely absent from the education of university physicians, even if some had begun advertising themselves as doctors 'of both medicines'. So, it comes about, says Thalhauser, 'that a barber, who has been a servant for a year or two, takes a wife and in one evening becomes a master surgeon'.[27]

Paracelsus had also observed this problem. In another book, written years before the one in which he included the Thalhauser letter, he scornfully asked artisan surgeons, 'if you are not a physician, what can you do other than work in the same way a tailor does'?[28] Healing required philosophical knowledge as a guide to knowing why a certain therapy or procedure should be done at all. The physician, Paracelsus says, 'recognizes the origin of illnesses, and practice guides the artisan surgeon.'[29] The medical art required the confluence of both theory and practice.

Given that it involved such fanfare, it seems truly odd that, in fact, the *Great Surgery* does not have much to do with surgery at all, being less concerned with procedures or even instruments than with the use of prepared medicines to treat wounds. There were very few surgical instruments in Paracelsus' possession at the time of his death, and despite his respect for certain well-practised wound physicians, there still remained a gap between surgical practice and his own medical world view. Surgical knowledge, like alchemical knowledge, was, however, part of the spectrum of craft experience – and, crucially, gaining such experience required the physician to travel, to be among those whom Paracelsus called the *perambulani* (wanderers). After all, he says, the arts have no feet; they won't come to you.[30] To learn the art thus meant joining a group that was hated and mocked by stay-at-home physicians, whose idea of travelling was to sit in the middle of their books and sail about in a ship of fools.[31] For Paracelsus, that kind of travelling was counterfeit and gave rise to a serious ethical problem. Despite boasting of possessing the kind of knowledge that could only come from real travelling and the pursuit of medical experience, these sedentary physicians were, in fact, not only unable to help their neighbours but were also bound to become miserly, hiding away, careful not to expose themselves and living off the credulity of others. God, however, had commanded otherwise. 'If we want to come to God,' Paracelsus writes, 'we have to go to him, for he says: come to me.'[32] The physician was obliged to find the gifts of God where He had placed them, for 'wisdom is a gift of God.'

Where God had disclosed different parts of the medical art, that is where, following the will of God, one had to discover them.[33] Doing so, Paracelsus knew, was not an easy road to travel. While the person who pursued the art ate milk soup, the stay-at-home physician ate partridges. From their chimney corners, they hated that which they were not, and the more they hated, the greedier they became. In his next defence, Paracelsus had a great deal to say to those who, while professing medicine, had forgotten their own souls for the sake of becoming rich.

FIVE

'I Am Ashamed of Medicine': Love, Labour and the Spirit of Christ in the Transformation of the Secular World

In a small book not published until well after his death, Paracelsus clearly expressed what he considered to be at the root of successful medical practice and what he held to be the ideal of the art of medicine. 'The bedrock of medicine,' he wrote,

> is love. To whatever extent there is love, that is what our prospects will be. If our love is great, what we do in medicine will be fruitful. Where it is lacking, whatever we attempt will be inadequate. For it is love that teaches the art. No true physician can be born without it.[1]

Love separated the true physician from the false. Without it, the art itself was defiled. The patient's suffering could not enter the physician's heart, and, like Christ himself, the art of medicine was betrayed for the sake of profit. There are two kinds of physicians, he declared, 'those who treat out of love, and [those who treat] out of self-interest and profit, and by their works both are known.'[2]

It is not just that one needs love to treat patients successfully; love is the key to understanding the secrets of nature and thus to becoming a knowledgeable and proficient doctor in the first place. Those who pursue these secrets as an act of love gain knowledge directly from God; to them God reveals the divine powers residing in the various parts of creation. Thus God, not a name, title or school, makes the physician. Loving God in the love of nature is what produces the ability to relieve a patient's suffering. By conveying confidence in the possession of those truths, the physician creates hope. In medicine, love makes hope through art.

Paracelsus knew that physicians followed no specific ethical rule, and in the fifth and sixth of the *Seven Defences*, he focused on the practices of false physicians, those who 'cripple and maim, sometimes strangling or even killing people, so that their own profit can be increased and not impeded'. He also shielded himself from those who had accused him of behaviour that was uncivil, coarse and lacking humility. In both defences, the issue is one of medical ethics and the grounds for distinguishing good and evil in a medical milieu whose only rule was 'take, take, whether or not it makes any sense', and in which 'each wants to use medicine but not know it.'[3] How some perceptions do linger: early in the twentieth century the Irish playwright and polemicist George Bernard Shaw (1856–1950), in the preface to a play first published in 1908, expressed similar criticisms and noted that the 'assent of the majority' was 'the only sanction known to [medical] ethics'. It was, he wrote, the 'sort of conscience' that equated to 'an intense dread of doing anything that everybody else does not do' and that 'makes it possible to keep order on a pirate ship'. Patients themselves, he quipped, were complicit in their own deception. When a loved one is sick and dying, we want something to be done, 'and the doctor does something. But sometimes what he does kills the patient', although 'he assures you that all that human skill could do has been done'. But no one, Shaw comments, 'has the brutality to say to the newly bereft father, mother, husband, wife, brother, sister, "you have killed your lost darling by your credulity."'[4] For Paracelsus, the problem of professional ethics related also to sociopolitical and religious thinking – indeed, social sentiments and religious beliefs pervade, like a universal ether, every part of his personal universe. Without recognizing the presence and relevance of Paracelsus' deep commitment to social and religious themes, his medical philosophy loses much of its personal meaning. When that happens, it changes into what we prefer to make of it and, as a consequence, gets lost in historical space.

There was really nothing revolutionary about the idea that love mattered in the practice of medicine. The Christian idea of *caritas*, associated with medieval cloister medicine, emphasized the love of the sick as a core value. As well as extending the idea to include a love of nature, Paracelsus was also able to list medical virtues he believed were prerequisites for utilizing medical skills in accordance with the will of God: 'The physician should be pure and chaste,' he asserts, and there should be 'no blemish of pride, envy, concupiscence, lack of chastity, arrogance, pomp, luxury, [false] respectability, vanity, or the like'.[5] This, he knew, did not correspond to the standard image of physicians, whose elevated social position was often reflected in rings, gold chains, furs and other finery. To Paracelsus, such sights were an abomination before God. Profit was the problem.

> It should not at all be surprising that I cannot extol profit in medicine. For because I know how very pernicious profit is in obstructing the arts, directing them only to pretense and purchase . . . which falsity causes corruption in all things, [I also know] that the physician should not grow from profit, but from love.[6]

Paracelsus predicted that people would think him crazy for saying such things:

> Now, when I explain the foundation of the physician to you in this way, you will surely say that I am out of my senses. No one will know what I am talking about. [People will say] I am possessed . . . [but] for the physician to be whole and stand on a complete foundation he must proceed . . . in accordance with the set order of nature, and not that of the human being.[7]

In the love of God and nature, one found what was pure. But, Paracelsus observed, to 'have compassion for one another, and fulfill the commandment to love' had by no means become a habit or custom. As he saw it, where all things should be done for love, physicians acted only for payment. Thus they had become 'thieves and murderers', their art nothing but 'babbling and quarreling'.[8]

What a paradox – denouncing the immorality of profit-oriented physicians but doing so in a manner that many thought arrogant and apparently lacking all humility. No one, his critics claimed, could do right by him. In response, Paracelsus acknowledged that he was not by nature 'subtly spun'. What he called silk others called coarse cloth. He had grown up, after all, not among women eating nice things like figs and wheat bread, but among pine cones, eating cheese and bread made of oats. The experiences of his youth had defined his life, and that had not made him into a refined fellow.[9] Those who thought themselves subtle and charming he thought were fakes, pretending a friendly and affectionate manner to dupe patients into spending money on useless medicine. Their medical practice was the product of human fantasy, and it had fallen to him to stir things up by telling the truth about it. In this, Paracelsus was not alone. The early sixteenth century, especially the 1520s, when he was frequently on the road, was a period of social, economic and religious rebellion, and Paracelsus' own revolt has to be understood as part of a much larger current of political and institutional unrest involving others whose habits seemed dangerous and strange – social revolutionaries and religious zealots among them.

From the perspective of a modern social-democratic state, the peasants of the area of southwestern Germany called Swabia were not asking for much. In a published document called the *Twelve Articles* (1525), they demanded, among other things, the right to choose and remove their own pastors, the reduction of tithes, hunting and fishing rights, the return to them of forests and pastures, the abolition of serfdom and death taxes, and restrictions on excessive labour. And yet Renaissance society was a world organized by rank and privilege. 'The heavens themselves, the planets, and this centre', Shakespeare purposefully wrote, 'Observe degree priority and place . . . Take but degree away, untune that string, and hark, what discord follows! Each thing meets in mere oppugnancy [an outbreak of violence]' (*Troilus and Cressida*, Act 1, Scene 3).

In early sixteenth-century Europe there was 'oppugnancy' aplenty. Luther had declared each person to be a priest unto himself, defying the scriptural authority of the Roman Catholic hierarchy – including the political and religious dominion of the Pope. In 1522 the lesser landholders (or 'knights') of the Rhineland rose up in revolt against an attempt by German princes to consolidate authority over feudal lands. Given the general aura of discontent and defiance of authority, the peasantry may have felt that their time had also come. Like Luther, they supported themselves with the Gospel. If any of the grievances set forth in the *Twelve Articles* should be found to be against the word of God by a clear explanation of scripture, they promised to withdraw it immediately. However, neither Luther, as we have seen, nor the Gospel would save them; and as thousands of peasants organized into armies all over the German-speaking areas of Central Europe, Catholic and Lutheran princes recognized a mutual peril. Peasants slaughtered landlords; mercenaries slaughtered peasants. Some of the fighting culminated in wholesale massacres as the German higher nobility, and the Holy Roman Empire (in the form of what was called the Swabian League) retaliated against the peasants. Thousands were killed, the insurrection mercilessly suppressed.

In the years surrounding the peasants' rebellion, Paracelsus found shelter in the episcopal city of Salzburg, a city ruled by a prince-archbishop. He rented an apartment (we know the street where he lived) and settled there for nearly two full years between 1524 and 1526. What brought him to the city is unclear, but he did have friends there. A few, as we have already seen, were connected to one of the city's famous baths, the Rappelbad. A few were learned men of the cloth, and we know that at one point Paracelsus exchanged ideas concerning matters of religion with several of them. One discussion, concerning the birth and sinless soul of Mary, mother of Jesus, especially attracted attention, and Paracelsus found himself invited to continue the discussion at the court of the Archbishop. He declined, excusing himself on the basis of his *stamelten Zunge* – literally, a 'stammering tongue', quite possibly a reference to his unsophisticated or insecure use of language. Talking to peasants in taverns, pubs and inns about religion was one thing, but engaging in debate at court was quite another. He promised to deliver his thoughts in writing.

Suddenly, in late spring 1526, Paracelsus disappeared, forsaking most of what he possessed and returning his apartment key not to the innkeeper but to the innkeeper's mother. He was in a hurry. A friend, Michael Setznagel, made a list of the things he left behind. There were a few pieces of furniture, 31 'small and large books' and a bunch of unbound texts. The list also included five 'fire benches' (or assaying ovens), four brass mortars, salves and vessels for making medicines. Finally, there was a broken wooden astrolabe and a projection on parchment of the world with the Sun and Moon. Paracelsus also left behind some of his clothes, including three coats lined with fur and a waistcoat made of damask. His innkeeper, Christoph Riss, took them home since Paracelsus still owed him money. Why the urgency? In this case, politics and religion were more the issue than medicine. Paracelsus had been writing treatises critical of religious ceremony and practices and had got himself caught up in a rebellion against the city's prince-archbishop, Matthäus Lang (1468–1540).[10] At court Paracelsus may well have been marked as a dangerous outsider, social renegade and heretic, and Lang knew how to deal with people like that.

Lang was a staunch defender of the Catholic faith and a sworn enemy of Protestant teachings. To many of the citizens of Salzburg, he was a ruthless and arrogant prince-archbishop, handing down summary justice on the peasants who defied his religious authority and forcing new taxes on the citizens of Salzburg to pay for personal luxuries. By 1525, in the middle of Paracelsus' residence in the city, nearly everybody had had enough. Miners, guilds, artisans and peasants joined forces and rejected the rule of the Archbishop altogether, seeking an end of governance by princes who were also prelates. By the end of May the town of Hallein, just south of Salzburg, was occupied. In early June the citizens of Salzburg opened the gates to an insurgent army, and Lang fled to his fortress, the Hohensalzburg. He stayed there for over two months, until, with the intervention of the Swabian League, an armistice ended hostilities. The guilds and artisans of Salzburg had made their point, or perhaps got their revenge. The archbishop returned to his residence, now a shambles.[11]

Some historians have attempted to establish a clear role for Paracelsus in the insurrection, but while some of those who took part were known to him, any direct participation on his part seems unlikely. There were plenty of reasons for him to be supportive of the revolt, however. His own developing religious views, some of which were expressed in writing while living in the city, mocked as idolatry the opulence and luxury of the courts of ecclesiastical princes like Lang, and surely the demands of peasants elsewhere for the abolition of serfdom and the free preaching of the Gospel would have resonated with his own private sentiments. While sympathetic, he needed to be careful. After all, as a bondsman of the abbey of Einsiedeln, he was not himself a free man, and he possessed no legal claim to the protections and civic rights afforded to Salzburg citizens. Once the insurgents were before the city gates, and with no certainty as to the outcome of the rebellion, friends may have encouraged him to leave town post-haste.

Good friends sometimes persuade you to stay, and sometimes they make sure that you go. Paracelsus' friends knew enough to perceive real personal danger in his expression of his medical, social and religious ideas. In conversations and private remarks, often in inns and taverns, what they heard was a message, expressed with religious intensity and biblical certainty, that foresaw a future in which the reform of medicine became part of the renewal of society. In this vision, labour not only perfected the physical world by means of craft, but perfected the human community as well.

Paracelsus' views harboured an enthusiasm for a blessed world comparable to that imagined by religious radicals, monastic mendicants and mystical prophets. The visions of these zealots were sometimes expressed in violent terms and with reference to the end of times and Armageddon. But it was not violence and abrupt rebellion that Paracelsus thought would bring such things about. He condemned war, censured both suicide and capital punishment, and kept himself apart from the terrors of the peasants' rebellion. And yet in one respect, the source of his views rested in the same perilous domain that animated more sweeping and ruthless protests. This was the notion, underlying claims to mystical experience, that God could speak directly and subjectively to prophets and ascetics, bypassing the established institutional framework of the Church. It amounted to a subjective theology of the inner voice, and as the world around Paracelsus was finding out, a theology of the inner voice, and the inspired fanaticism that resulted, could be very dangerous.

One person to whom God spoke directly in the mid-1530s was a charismatic preacher named Jan van Leiden (1509–1536). He sought a renewal of society in the German city of Münster, seeking to outlaw money and the possession of private property, and proclaiming polygamy as necessary to social equality. Joining other inspired preachers, Jan van Leiden established this theocracy in Münster and promised salvation to all those who acknowledged him as the city's prophet king. The prophet kingdom, however, did not last long. It came to an end in 1535 following a siege by a Catholic army in the service of the territorial bishop. Jan van Leiden was tortured and finally executed. To make a point about rebellion against established authority, officials left his body and those of his close supporters unburied, suspending them in metal cages from the tower of Münster's St Lambert's church. The bones were removed several decades later, but the cages are still there today.

In the early 1520s an earlier enthusiast for the inner covenant of the heart, a radical preacher named Thomas Müntzer (1489–1525), became a leader of peasants in the German duchy of Thuringia. His inspired message was not subtle:

> I tell you that the time has come for bloodshed to fall upon the impenitent world for its unbelief . . . One knows full well and can prove it with Scripture that lords and princes . . . are not Christians. Your priests and monks pray to the devil . . . all your preachers are hypocrites.[12]

The inner voice demanded carnage, but the real slaughter to follow was of the peasants themselves. Before long Müntzer would also be no more, tortured and executed on 27 May 1525, just as guilds, artisans, miners and peasants were coming closer to their own rebellion in Salzburg. During his brief residency in that city, Paracelsus had increasingly joined his medical philosophy to a vision of a reformed society in which the fruits of the earth could be shared by all.

It was fortunate for Paracelsus that his friends were so considerate of him, because Paracelsus was, above all, an emphatic individualist. In his religious beliefs as well as in his sociopolitical views, he remained always his own man. The results could be confusing and seem contradictory. He criticized the outward rituals and some of the beliefs of the Catholic Church and accused bishops, clerics and monks 'who guzzled wine and attended to whores' of promoting wholesale murder rather than relying upon Christian teaching in responding to the expansion of the Turkish (Ottoman) empire.[13] Yet, for all the complaint, he died a Catholic. He promoted views based in his own conscience but admitted that institutional structures came from God. Concentrated in some specific texts and scattered throughout his writings are engagements with questions concerning the correct use of riches and the ethics of labour and profit. He predicted the end of the inequitable social order he saw around him, and the coming into being of a communal society; but he saw the means to that end not in revolution but in the apparatus of existing governments. These things certainly seemed strange, but, after all, as he said in the sixth of his *Seven Defences*, he was known for his 'strange manner'. What would be regarded as most strange was yet to come.

The passage from Paul's first letter to Corinthians, 'When the perfect is come, the imperfect will pass away' (1 Corinthians 13:10), had been given apocalyptic interpretations more than once and had inspired sanctified visions of abrupt change in the future. For Paracelsus, however, changing the social order was a process in time, historical time; and like any process was subject to human desire and dexterity. The true Christian community, where each member was part of a brotherhood in the body of Christ, had to be built, and it is one of the most curious aspects of his social/religious thinking that, as a result of that view, Paracelsus considered poverty to be a special, even holy, calling. Poverty was, therefore, not a failing, but the locus of human action that, over time, manifested true Christian kinship and solidarity. The poor were closest to God because in poverty, all were equal; without the poor, there could be no completion by human moral initiative of what was incomplete and imperfect in the social order. In alchemical terms, from the social dross of poverty, the spiritual and moral work of the Christian community extracted the spirit of Christ. In turn, by means of projection, this would permeate the public sphere, bringing into being an equitable social order.

One idea for setting such a process in motion was to reconsider the relationship between labour and material wealth such that property and the profits derived from production could be shared by an entire community. The human being was a custodian of the material world, and his goods belonged not just to him but also to his neighbour. What Paracelsus had in mind was a restructuring of the social hierarchy traditionally referred to as the 'estates'. In that system, a small part of society – namely, the nobility and upper clergy, whose status was most often inherited – lived off the productions of rural and urban labour. Paracelsus imagined a new social order in which labour of various kinds (related to agriculture, craftsmanship, practical–theoretical learning and sociopolitical administration) created social categories that served the well-being of all. His was to be a community of production in which 'he who has much comes to the aid of he who has nothing'. In that community, a person's labour could not be possessed by anyone else. It and it alone was the source of genuine wealth, the type of wealth that benefited one's neighbour and accomplished the completion of a Christian ideal.[14]

Labour and the family were at the core of this ideal. To support labour and its rigours, Paracelsus thought that a four-day work week would be sufficient, since 'holy work' was not oriented towards profit but rather towards providing the necessities of life. In writing about marriage, he insisted upon absolute monogamy and the necessity of an unbreakable bond between parents and their children in which children bore the duty of obedience and parents shouldered the responsibility of educating their sons and daughters. Education was key to completing the perfection of the human and physical world, and in emphasizing the notion of completing creation through education, Paracelsus reflected an idea that might be considered profound. Far from being an original idea, this notion was, in fact, very old. Closer to the time of Paracelsus, it was revised by an Italian scholar who died very young named Giovanni Pico della Mirandola (1463–1494). It is the idea that the human being stands at the centre of creation with one foot in the material world and one in the world of spirit or intellect. He or she is both a part of nature and is able to observe nature. The human being provides the means by which nature comes to reflect upon its own existence, is able to think about itself, to know itself. Through the human being, nature becomes self-conscious. This gives the human being enormous dignity, and the responsibility of education becomes a responsibility of cosmic and divine proportions.

Some studies of Paracelsus have linked ideas like this to early Christian thinking. This is not surprising because, along with an exposure to medicine and nature provided by his father, Paracelsus also received a comprehensive, biblically based religious education. He was raised amid religious rites and practices, visited cloister schools as a boy, learnt Catholic dogma and was enmeshed in daily religious observance. Among those from whom he had received spiritual tutoring in early life, either directly or indirectly, were bishops and abbots who possessed local and regional reputations. Several are mentioned in his book on surgery, the *Grossen Wundartznei*, among them Bishop Matthias Scheit (*c.* 1440–1512), a man already known to Paracelsus' father, who had collected a valuable library of juridical and theological books. There was also the suffragan of Passau, Nikolaus Kaps, who taught at the University of Vienna in 1495; and the polymath Abbot Johannes Trithemius (1462–1516) – although his actual influence and identity is a matter of some contention among Paracelsus scholars – whose library was also vast and whose own interests extended to occult studies and cryptography.

In his early twenties, Paracelsus had turned his attention to religious themes, debating with common people concerning fasting, confessing and taking the sacraments, and composing polemical works that were critical of the Church.[15] Two of his most interesting and potentially dangerous texts were apparently written down during his time in Salzburg.[16] One was called *Liber de sancta trinitate* (A Book Concerning the Holy Trinity) and the other *De septem punctis idolatriae christianae* (Concerning Seven Points of Christian Idolatry) – either one would have raised eyebrows and likely have caught the attention of the archbishop. Paracelsus viewed their content as consistent with traditional Catholic teaching and practice, but for others, they aroused suspicions of heresy. The fact that he readily admitted that he spoke of his religious criticisms in taverns was also a point of rebuke. Authorities told him to sit down and shut up. He did neither, and in the process converted tavern talk into a firm demand for religious reform.

He addressed the theologians who had demeaned him directly:

> Your daily hostility and scurrilous tirades against me have been on account of me speaking the truth, things that I have sometimes discussed in taverns, pubs, and inns when arguing against the useless churchgoing, lavish celebrations, fruitless praying and fasting, alms giving, sacrifices, tithing . . . taking the sacrament and all the other commands of priests and demands for their own upkeep. And you have said that these things took place while I was drunk and in a tavern. Of course taverns are supposed to be good-for-nothing places for the display of truth, and on that account you have called me a hole-in-the-wall preacher [*Winkelprediger*].[17]

Earlier, when he had endorsed what the priests wanted to hear – namely, that one should make sacrifices and follow

17 Lay preaching, from Hartmann Schedel, *Liber chronicarum* (Nuremberg Chronicle, 1493).

what the priests said – talking in taverns was fine. But if it had been fine then, Paracelsus argued, those same priests should accept the truth of the tavern now:

> For in those bars I was credulous on your behalf, but now I am faithful to Christ and no longer believe in you. And so, if several of you came into a tavern with me I would tell people: protect yourself from these false prophets and frauds. They're sent by the Devil.[18]

The cultural, religious and political event that we have come to know as the Protestant Reformation – in which Paracelsus played his own small part – was well under way by the 1520s.[19] But already some reformers had begun to disagree with others. A split between Luther and the Swiss reformer Ulrich Zwingli developed as a result of different notions concerning the presence of Christ in the Eucharist. For Paracelsus, none of the religious alternatives sufficiently embraced his own philosophical and religious views. The Lutherans, Zwinglians, Anabaptists and Papists were, for him, 'four pairs of trousers made of one cloth'.[20] In religion, as in life, Paracelsus was homeless and wandering – alone and adrift, yet forever true to himself. Perhaps it is for this reason that his written polemics and criticisms against the Roman Catholic Church were, in some ways, even more sweeping and profound than the censures of Luther or Zwingli. In one text, his *Seven Points of Christian Idolatry*, he separated the church made of walls – the institutional church – from the church as constituted by the Holy Spirit. The church with walls was, regrettably, the church to which most people belonged; for Paracelsus, it was bound up with pageantry, worldly power and wealth, the works of the Devil. Going to that church was of no use, he said, and should be forbidden. He also condemned the ritual of confessing sins. This, he argued, was altogether hypocritical, since forgiveness could be gained without true contrition. To be truly contrite involved only one thing: performing the only act of sincere contrition, the only thing that really mattered in the sight of God – divesting yourself of all property by giving to the poor.

This voluntary impoverishment was just the beginning. Certain types of prayer should also be curtailed, Paracelsus argued, especially that of priests and monks, whose prayers went on for hours and amounted to 'the living voice of the Devil'.[21] Real prayer expressed the needs of the soul and was best carried in one's heart.

> Concerning prayer, it is a work of the devil that someone having said a rosary should have more in heaven than someone with a *Pater Noster* (the Lord's Prayer) and someone who sings should have more than the person who mutters. All of it is heretical nonsense and contrary to Christ. [This is] total idolatry.[22]

The Lord's Prayer was a concentrated form of a very personal, altogether internalized, act of belief. You did not need a church of walls for that.

Another point of idolatry related to the culture of holy days and the related practices that, Paracelsus claimed, took up almost a third of the entire year. Celebrations were fine, but no one got to heaven because of them. The same for fasting:

if you want to purify the body, go ahead and fast, he says, but it would be an error to think that fasting makes one more pleasing to God. Faith rests in a person regardless of whether he or she is fasting or well fed; and despite the acts of apparent sacrifice, there was room for faith even in a murderer, thief or traitor.[23] Almsgiving was also useless as a means of arousing God's special favour. Alms should be given to the needy out of love, never as a means of obtaining love. From this it followed that all the alms that one gave to the cloisters were given to the Devil, because such gifts were given for the purpose of spiritual recompense and reward. Giving alms at the church door also missed its mark, since those alms did not, as they were intended, feed the poor and hungry. It was an illusion to think they did. In reality, they only served to feed the whores of priests and the priests' illegitimate children.[24]

As Lucifer had constructed a cult in heaven, so the papacy had done on earth. In fact, in Rome Lucifer reigned as Pope. His army consisted of the monks, nuns, priests, spiritual knights and religious orders. The entire world of Catholic observances and sacramentals was also a sham – laying the cross on the dying, the reverence of the cross and the saints, relics, holy water, the blessing of the fruits of the earth, all of it was diabolical because all of it was directed toward outward appearance. For Paracelsus, none of it had the slightest connection to the inwardness of faith, nor did the altars, pulpits, bishops' mitres and priestly vestments of the Catholic Church. True faith had no need of such decorations.

> The temple of God lies in the heart, not in stone and mortar. Adornments are to be found in faith, not on

> walls or altars; blessings reside in love, not in the hands. Hands were created for labour, not for blessing. Use that member [the hands] that God has given you to feed yourself, not for benedictions. Use it instead in the fields, not for driving out the devil. Drive him out with your faith, not with exorcisms and conjuring, not with words and fists.[25]

Images were worst of all. No Christian, he thought, should pray before an image, for 'in all images is idolatry'.[26] Pictures in books were fine, however, as long as they were not made objects of prayer.

Catholic theology demanded participation in the sacraments, and if Paracelsus was rejecting every practice and symbol of Church authority, it was because for him, as for Luther and other reformers, salvation followed from an internal faith, a trust in God that required no institutional acts of veneration. As he wrote, 'if the basis of righteousness should be regarded and maintained, each should know to seek salvation internally, not externally. Whoever cuts himself off from righteousness, does so internally.'[27] Salvation was a matter of the heart, and had nothing to do with rituals involving the body: 'Believe only that the Holy Spirit baptizes you. For every human being is his own prince, his own king and master, to command himself.'[28] Salvation resulted from faith, not sacraments, and, most important, with true faith came also the desire to comfort the poor.

> Now, only Christ is the father of salvation, not man; and so how may one be saved who has another father

> who himself is not saved? That is to say, we must follow Christ [our saviour] by forsaking all our property and giving it to the poor. Why do the vestments, the mitre and staff, the silk trousers . . . and other things still remain? Christ says to sell everything . . . Seeking salvation [means that] you lords of all the estates [must] follow Christ and give away all your goods, otherwise there is no salvation for you, however much you live according to the law, however obedient, or pious, all of it is nothing but error.[29]

Paracelsus certainly knew the Bible, and his writings are strewn with biblical references. He wrote commentaries on the Old and New Testaments and addressed specific themes like baptism and repentance. He even took up one of the central issues of reformation theology – namely, the issue of whether Christ was physically present in the Eucharist. He wrote sermons, fashioning himself as a kind of lay preacher, addressing whomever would listen. Most striking, however, are his ideas concerning the structure of the Trinity, the notion central to Christian doctrine that three divine persons – Father, Son and Holy Spirit – coexist as one God. In Paracelsus' thinking, the Trinity takes an unusual turn, because God the Father, in order to produce God the Son, needed a female, heavenly spouse.

The idea is explained most clearly in a little essay called *A Book Concerning the Holy Trinity*, a text almost entirely unknown until rediscovered and published for the first time in the twentieth century. The idea was radical to say the least, and Paracelsus was accused of believing in both a male and female deity. His reasoning, however, was far more subtle, and was carefully structured to avoid hypostatizing four persons rather than three. God the Father, he writes, 'divided his person into two persons, and yet it remained in one divinity . . . [He then] separated from himself a woman so that he and she [although two persons] are only one God.'[30] However you slice it, this heavenly woman and divine spouse of God the Father is a goddess, necessary for creating the Son of God.

Even for the Godhead, Paracelsus argued, creation involved separation; and separation was equally the key term in understanding how creation worked in the natural world. The separation of light from darkness was the first act of physical creation, and Paracelsus describes how, by means of his divine Word, God also separated from himself the dynamic and spiritual beginnings of nature – the *Yilastrum*, a formless, unknowable and all-powerful matter that was the spiritual origin of all things. Within the *Yilastrum*, the *tria prima* (the three principles of physical being – Sulphur, Salt and Mercury) became the elementary wombs of physical being and established the link between spiritual and material bodies. In turn, natural bodies arose from what Paracelsus called the *limbus terrae*, a purified extract separated from all the elements. This formed the macrocosm and, when endowed with a sidereal spirit and a divine soul, the human being. So, the being of the human being was threefold: a combination of body, soul and spirit. Made of all of nature, the human being carried the world within as a microcosm of creation. Made of Sulphur, Salt and Mercury, composed of soul, body and spirit, he or she was a world within a world that was elementary, sidereal and eternal. From this emerged sense and thought, the recognition of good and evil and, by means of knowledge, the means to complete creation as part of creation, to perfect nature as part of nature and to become finally nature's way of knowing why there is anything at all.

SIX

Invisible Beings and Invisible Diseases: Magic and Insanity in an Age of Faith

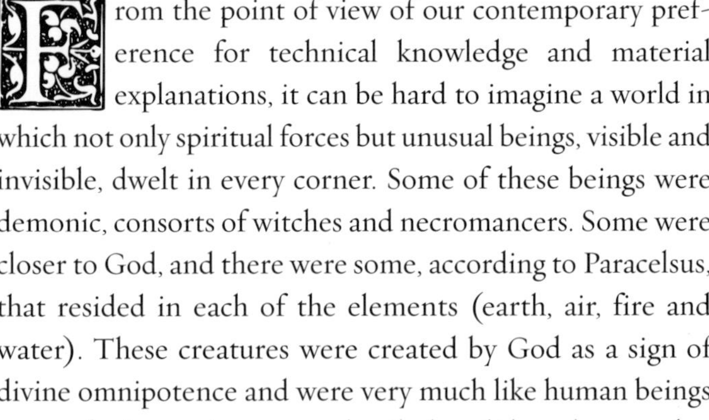

From the point of view of our contemporary preference for technical knowledge and material explanations, it can be hard to imagine a world in which not only spiritual forces but unusual beings, visible and invisible, dwelt in every corner. Some of these beings were demonic, consorts of witches and necromancers. Some were closer to God, and there were some, according to Paracelsus, that resided in each of the elements (earth, air, fire and water). These creatures were created by God as a sign of divine omnipotence and were very much like human beings except for in one important detail: they did not have souls.

What Paracelsus called 'pygmies' or 'gnomi' lived in the earth. They were the most subtle of all the elementary spirits since they moved through solid rock. What air was to human beings, the earth was to the gnomi. The beings that lived in fire were called 'salamanders', and those that lived in air were 'sylphs'. 'Nymphs' lived in water. Each had its own society and laws, wore clothes and produced children. Sometimes, however, what they produced were monsters – sirens, dwarfs, giants and will-o'-the-wisps. Each day Paracelsus awoke to surroundings packed with forces, powers and beings that did not fit into the realms of animal, vegetable or mineral. When encountering such beings, he knew to be careful. After all, the elementary spirits were eager to acquire souls, and there was only one way to do so – by marrying a human. Then they and their children, possessing souls, could obtain salvation.

While most of these beings languished in their respective elements, nymphs were known to leave theirs and become visible. They could often be seen sitting on the banks of brooks, Paracelsus explained, and when visible, could co-habit with humans. If, however, you were attracted to one and happened to fall in love, you had better be on your guard. Nymphs liked water and once married (and in possession of a soul) might disappear back into the water if a spouse was not watchful. But while a nymph might vanish, the spouse's marital promise remained inviolable. Paracelsus tells the story of an unfortunate German nobleman named Peter Dimringer von Staufenberg who lived with a nymph and then repudiated her, calling her a devil, and took another wife. This was a grave mistake, and von Staufenberg was dead shortly after his wedding, killed by the nymph whom he had abused. Shocking as this retribution may be, to Paracelsus, the act was altogether justified. Since she was not protected by human law, he argued, and because the world now falsely repudiated her as a devil, God had granted her the right to carry out a punishment appropriate to her husband's adultery.[1]

As von Staufenberg discovered, spirits – in this case, an elementary spiritual creature – could do great harm. But other kinds of spirits – ones that could not be defined as beings or creatures but rather were astral powers and chemical vapours

– were also at work every minute of every day in the human world, posing their own threats to one and all. Some of these, as we have seen, caused physical ailments. Others were the source of ailments of a psychic kind, something akin to madness. These, Paracelsus admitted, may be curable or may not be.

Some doctors had accused him of not knowing immediately what ailed a patient, and therefore of not being able to provide straightaway what each patient needed or desired. In the last of his *Seven Defences*, he acknowledged that not every illness could be cured – this was simply not within his or anyone else's power, since no one could overpower the will of God. The most difficult to treat were diseases that were, as he says, hidden by a curtain that was near impossible to see through.[2] Among these were invisible diseases that related to the sufferings of the mind.

For Paracelsus, the human being was a beast with intellect and a soul. He or she possessed a physical body but also a spriritual or celestial body that accounted for reason, art, wisdom and craft. However, because everything in the microcosm was also found in the macrocosm, celestial influences also brought about unreason and disorder. That relationship, essential for what we might call his theory of mental illness, is a central concern of one of Paracelsus' most important books. It was only partially completed, parts of it written down in 1537 while Paracelsus was treating a severely ill patient in a small Bohemian town called Mährisch-Kromau (now Moravský Krumlov, Czech Republic). The fragments came into print, collected with other miscellania, in a volume that appeared thirty years after his death. The book is sometimes called the *Philosophia sagax* (Clear-sighted Philosophy), sometimes the *Astronomia magna* (Great Astronomy). Regardless of how we refer to it, this is a book about the powers of the heavens and the ways those powers both caused diseases and might be used to cure them – including diseases of the human spirit, or madness. Another of his books stands out even more prominently in regard to these questions: a short text published first in 1567 (again, years after Paracelsus' death) called *Schreyben von den Kranckheyten so die Vernunfft Berauben* (Diseases that Rob a Person of Reason). In it, he described in detail the causes of madness across several categories. He first accounted for the causes of epilepsy and mania and then turned his attention to the origins of the sufferings of those he called insane. The insane, he said, were of four types: *lunatici*, *insani*, *vesani* and *melancholici*.

What was experienced as an earthquake in the macrocosm, Paracelsus explained, the individual microcosm experienced as epilepsy. Both were caused by a vapour arising from a specific spirit (he called it the *spiritus vitae*) that made the whole body, terrestrial or human, tremble. It was similar, he explained, to what happened when 'a piece of sodium . . . falls into vinegar [and] makes everything boil'.[3] Depending on where this vapour occurred (brain, liver, heart, intestines or limbs, for example), specific symptoms would follow. If it occurred in the head, 'unconsciousness and insensitiveness result and carry away all reason'.[4] What Paracelsus called mania, on the other hand – a condition manifesting as frantic behaviour, unreasonableness, constant restlessness and mischieviousness – arose from distillations and sublimations in the body that produced vapours affecting the body's different parts. Mania, in other words, was the result of chemical processes, and, as such, the spirits involved could be described in mechanical terms. The body's own sublimations and distillations created matter that was 'so fine and sharp' that 'by touching the particles of the brain', it would cloud the cells of reason.[5] This may not sound like a revolutionary claim, but it is significant nevertheless. Rather than tracing the cause of mania to diabolical possession, Paracelsus claimed a physical link, and physical causes allow for physical – that is, medical or pharmaceutical – cures. Yet even this proved controversial in the long run. While it did mark a step away from ascribing mental afflictions to the malevolence of demons and witches, locating the origin of perceived mental disorder in specific functions or parts of the body opened another can of worms. Some physicians, even in the nineteenth and twentieth centuries, believed that mental illness was itself a consequence of troublesome anatomy. Among the procedures developed in line with this theory – and which became accepted parts of informed, standard medical practice – were the extraction of teeth, the removal of parts of the bowel and, in women, cliterectomies and oophorectomies. In the late Renaissance several artists satirized the notion of physical causes of madness, depicting surgeons cutting open patients to remove a fantasized 'stone of madness' (illus. 18).

In Paracelsus' view, those who suffered from mania were not really insane, since the cause of their disease could be corrected by means of chemical medicines. Among those who are truly insane, he noted, 'some lose their reason and then regain it', and some remained without reason until they died.[6] Over two centuries later, one of the most important figures in the history of psychiatry, William Battie (1703–1776), distinguished between two sorts of insanity in a little book attacking the custodians of the Bedlam hospital. His *Treatise on Madness* (1758) distinguished between a form of madness present since birth (which he called 'original madness') and a form of madness that occurred as a result of experiences in life, especially as a result of emotional and physical trauma. This latter he called 'consequential madness'. Where original madness might be incurable, those who suffered from consequential madness might well respond to therapies and healing regimens. Paracelsus made a similar distinction. Rather than being simply locked away as incurable, some people could recover from what was really a physical illness. The key was understanding the chemistry of the body.

Among the diseases that robbed people of their reason, Paracelsus also included categories linked to both the womb and to the stars. Those he labelled *lunatici* suffered from the influence of the Moon. 'The stars', he noted, 'have the power to hurt and weaken our body and to influence health and illness. They . . . influence reason invisibly and insensibly, like a magnet attracting iron.' Just as the Sun could extract the humidity from the Earth, the Moon's power of attraction 'tears reason out of man's head by depriving him of humors and cerebral virtues'.[7]

Those called *insani* received insanity in the womb, the result of faulty seed (*sperma*) that lacked sufficient power to build a healthy brain. As with the madness of the *lunatici*, the Moon might play a role here, too, albeit a different one: 'If, at its height, the power of attraction of the moon interferes with the generation and conception of the child,' Paracelsus

explains, then 'the moon can take away reason, so that complete sanity can never be restored.'[8] In some cases, alchemically prepared quintessences of such things as gold, pearls, silver, corals, antimony and vitriol might help. The best solution, however, was not to treat but to prevent insanity – and here Paracelsus suggested what most of us would find a disturbing regimen.

Insanity originating in the womb, he explained, was already hidden in the intense bestial desire for coitus. So having sex when you passionately desired it provided an opportunity for a form of fervent insanity to be passed to any child conceived in such a manner. Paracelsus' message is clear: do not have sex when you feel the keen desire for it. Indeed, only have

18 Pieter Huys, *A Surgeon Extracting the Stone of Folly*, c. 1561, oil on wood.

sex when the natural desire has been extinguished (Paracelsus suggests jumping into cold water). But even this is not enough. To be absolutely sure that insanity will not begin in the womb, Paracelsus suggests having sex artificially – that is, by means of inducing desire (and the ability to perform sexually) through pharmacy, specifically by means of alchemically prepared quintessences. 'Thus, whenever one has the desire for coitus, it should be incited by medicine.' Such a regimen is especially important if those who are already insane want to have sex. 'It should be remembered', he writes, 'that insane persons must be prepared by means of quintessence before coitus. In this way the genital organs are protected against things unsuitable and inconvenient, so that no evil birth or insanity may result.'[9]

Sex and madness were also connected in Paracelsus' description of the third group of the insane, those he calls *vesani*. In a religious sense, this form of insanity followed from the sinful, bestial nature of the human being overwhelming the part of the person that was spiritual and divine. Madness was a form of inebriation. Some lost their reason, Paracelsus observed, through an excess of eating or drinking, and there was in his description of how this occurred a clearly expressed sexual element. 'It often happens', he says, 'that food offered by whores causes deprivation of the senses . . . Such insanity may lead to love, so that the *vesani* put all their being into whores.' Bestial natures were clearly prone to culinary love potions, he writes, and that one could come across 'those that have so eaten and drunk that they . . . are compelled to love a woman'. He quickly warns us, however, that, if a person is choleric (prone to anger) by nature, attempts to induce love through ingestion of food and drink risks having the opposite effect. In such cases, people 'are bent on war only' and there is 'no sanity' discernible.[10]

Among the fourth and final group that Paracelsus singles out, the *melancholici*, there is no defect in reason; rather it is that reason and memory become suppressed. In an explanation clearly connected to ancient traditions, Paracelsus explains the condition as a predisposition towards certain humoral complexes that can be affected by a variety of external and internal factors. The notion stands squarely in the tradition of Hippocratic medicine, and Paracelsus not only admits the relevance of thinking in terms of Hippocratic humours as causing melancholy, but accepts (albeit with a twist) the ancient view that the best treatment is by means of contraries. If a patient were too boisterous or laughing too much, a sad medicine is required. If the melancholic patient is despondent, a happy alchemical medicine, like *aurum potabile* (drinkable gold), will make him well again. 'Thus, the reason is set free and the memory is completely normal.'[11]

Further on in the same text Paracelsus singled out special illnesses for specific attention. One is what was called St Vitus's dance. The cause of the disease, he believed, was found in both the body and, importantly, the imagination. On the one hand, opening certain veins (Paracelsus called them 'laughing veins') so stirred the spirit in the blood that a relentless tickling sensation resulted in certain parts of the body, causing uncontrolled laughter and other outbursts. A person might continue laughing until he died if bleeding from that vein continued. The other cause, however, was related to the way that imagination was affected by 'reckless and disgraceful living'. This was one of the reasons why, he explained, prostitutes and scoundrels 'who satisfy all voluptuousness, bodily pleasure, imagination and fancy' never escape the disease, but dance, howl, scream and jump around as if lacking all reason.'

Common people considered such recklessness of the mind to be a plague sent by St Vitus, but it was, Paracelsus insisted, nothing more than 'an imaginative sickness'. If caused naturally – that is, if rooted in the 'laughing veins' – Paracelsus recommended a mixture of different medicines (*aurum potabile; mandragora*, or essence of opium) and a salve that was to be rubbed on the place of greatest ticklishness. If it was a lascivious disease, characterized by a 'voluptuous urge to dance' (more common in women than in men, 'since women have more imagination'), he recommended the oppositional approach of shutting 'the patients in a dark, unpleasant place', letting them fast on bread and water 'so that the lasciviousness is driven out by abstinence'.[12] For those afflicted with a recklessness of mind as a result of rage, the recommended therapy worked by means of sympathetic magic.

> The patient should make a likeness of himself in wax or resin, and should concentrate on it so that all the curses he has uttered may be destroyed in that likeness by his will . . . and then he should cast it into the fire, letting it burn completely so that neither ashes nor smoke shall remain.[13]

In this way, argued Paracelsus, thoughts are destroyed along with the poppet doll, as they are linked by the power of the imagination.

The imagination was a powerful thing, forming a bridge between the mind and the body. The sixteenth-century French physician Ambroise Paré noted examples of pregnancies gone bad, including an instance of a woman giving birth to a hairy child after having concentrated during conception on an image of John the Baptist depicted with long hair, a beard and wearing skins. Another woman Paré describes giving birth to a child with the face of a frog after holding a frog (a folk remedy for curing a fever) during sex.[14] For Paracelsus, the imagination was a kind of craftsman, possessing 'both the art and the entire equipment to make everything that it has in mind', whether it be a painting, a weaving, something made of metal or a child:

> The child that lies within the mother is her soil and sphere . . . the woman [operating] within her imagination is the craftsman and . . . the child is the ground upon which the work is carried out.[15]

What a woman saw or experienced during conception, Paracelsus agreed, would be the image drawn onto the fruit of her own body. In men, the imagination – especially of those who 'whore around in their senses and thoughts' – produced a kind of unnatural *sperma*, usually at night, during sleep. Paracelsus called it a stale salt and explained how it was carried away by spirits of the night who would use it to make monsters whenever they could also 'find a womb to serve their purpose'. If that happened, and if the gestation was brought to term, the issue 'was nothing human with a soul'. No one could know what birth would result, only that it would be contrary to the natural order. Even so, combinations of *sperma*, natural and unnatural, sometimes took place. In such cases, Paracelsus insisted, 'these abortive creatures are not less human, as unpleasing as they may look.'[16]

Imagination and madness would continue to be seen as going hand in hand. Centuries later the famous English poet and critic Samuel Johnson (1709–1784) observed of the imagination that '[when] fictions begin to operate as realities, false opinions fasten upon the mind, and life passes in dreams of rapture or of anguish.'[17] Some thought that illusions and dreams were the work of the Devil – people could be demonically possessed, after all – but others believed that religion was itself a factor in causing madness. The English poet and physician Richard Blackmore (1654–1729) identified acute melancholy with the imaginations of religious persons overly concerned about their eternal fates. Paracelsus would have agreed. While the Devil could also take possession of the soul and produce madness, too much religion, he thought, could really make you sick – indeed, in a little book called *De causis morborum invisibilium* (Concerning the Causes of Invisible Illnesses), Paracelsus connected religious thinking and madness, noting how faith could be used as a weapon to cause harm to others.

A physician, he says, can use his medications either to help or to kill a patient. Likewise, human beings, through the power of faith, were capable of visiting good or evil upon someone else. Faith was a form of magic and worked, for good or ill, invisibly over distances. 'You are of course visible and corporeal. But there is another who is also you who is not visible. What your body does this other one does as well. You do it visibly, the other invisibly.'[18] This invisible counterpart, which each human being has, could, Paracelsus claimed, be sent out to do good or evil:

> For we become [by way of faith] just like those spirits to which all things are possible and that can do the things invisibly which the body does visibly . . . By virtue of our intense faith, people can be put to death by prayer, [or made] crippled and lame.[19]

The faith that came from Christ and that was the means to salvation could thus be abused. Part of that abuse, a form of madness in itself, were the false beliefs that manifested themselves in enthusiastic religious practices. Saints became idols and their relics the source of insane superstitions as men whittled images and prayed to them as 'wooden gods'. Belief, however, formed and fashioned the world, and some beliefs actually created illnesses. It was possible, he argued, for a person to believe himself so ardently to be possessed that he could be become so by the very intensity of the pretence. Others, described by Paracelsus as those with obstinate and inflated minds, might seize upon some biblical verse and invest it with such a powerful belief that they became overwhelmed by the force of their belief and were willing to die for it. Paracelsus had a particular religious sect in mind, a group that insisted upon adult baptism and seemed to thrive on persecution. These were the Anabaptists, or 'rebaptizers', a group despised for both religious and social reasons by Catholics and Protestants alike. Their members expressed, Paracelsus declared, a 'mad faith', obstinately pursuing martyrdom for the sake of their baptismal convictions. But such fanatical commitment to religious belief ignored the true purpose of a Christian life as Paracelsus had defined it. If everyone sought death the way they did on the basis of such a mad faith, he observed, 'then no one who suffers hunger would be fed, no one naked be clothed, no one sick made well.'[20]

At the beginning of his little book about invisible diseases, Paracelsus noted once again the central role of the human being in understanding the wonders – both visible and invisible – of nature. We are commanded, he says, to understand the works of the Creator. Nature and her powers exist, in fact, so that we can trace God's 'deep and unfathomable wisdom'. Our role in creation is to explore 'the wondrous things in his mysteries', not only to satisfy ourselves 'but also to make his great wonders manifest . . . For we are not born to doze but rather to be awake and alert to all his works.'[21] For most modern readers, the claim that there is a duty to inquire into the powers of nature will most readily signal a scientific enterprise. However, what Paracelsus is insisting upon is the relevance of and duty to study something else – namely, the controversial notion of understanding and manipulating nature in terms of magic. Wherever one looks in his writings – be they about disease, wounds, medicines, natural philosophy, the powers of the heavens or good and evil spirits – the subject of magic, understood as an awareness and control of hidden mysteries, is close at hand.

Various sorts of magic coexisted in the Renaissance, each staking a claim to possessing and directing natural and supernatural powers. Some forms were diabolical, some astral and others natural. Discussion about which was which became a major topic of debate and led to bitter confrontations. Paracelsus would have known of the writings of the most well-known Renaissance writers on magic. Especially important would have been the texts of two writers: Marsilio Ficino (1433–1499) and Cornelius Agrippa (1486–1535). For Ficino, everything that existed was thoroughly saturated with spirit. There existed, he argued, an *anima mundi* or 'world soul' that was concentrated in the Sun and that influenced all the parts of the world by means of an astral fifth essence. Ficino described the work of the *magus* (magician) as attracting and intensifying astrological powers by means of making talismans – that is, by engraving images and symbols on certain metals that corresponded to the planets. He warned, however, that a maker of talismans had to be careful not to attract demons instead of planetary influences. One never knew for sure what might get attracted to a talisman, since, in the super-saturated spiritual cosmos between the material world and the divine, there existed eshelons of angels, demons and intelligences, as well as the astral powers. Nevertheless, for Ficino, the human being was the meeting place of a material body and a rational soul and thus was capable of not only establishing, by means of magic, a relationship between one thing in nature and another, but of making use of the hidden powers of the stars to manipulate these things.

For both Ficino and Agrippa, magic had ancient origins. Agrippa, however, divided the world of magic into parts that were elemental (that is, material), celestial (astrological and mathematical) and intellectual (the realm of demons and angels). Each was closely associated with the others as powers passed from their divine origin through the ranks of angels and demons, through the celestial bodies and into the world of material things. By means of symbols (letters, words, numbers and images), the *magus* could connect to the spiritual powers represented by them and bring about effects in the natural world. This was a special sort of word magic that followed from a holy magical wisdom called Cabala, an esotericism which in the Renaissance was given a Christianized form based on the ancient Judaic Kabbalah. If properly prepared through prayer, good works and purification of the mind, the *magus* could, many thought, summon angels and other good spirits. He could then perform works that seemed miraculous, compelling spirits, stars and the elements to obey his command (illus. 19).

Paracelsus accepted entirely the existence of demons and witches, and acknowledged their power to do great harm. Witches gained their power by turning away from God, and Paracelsus considered them to be among the most evil beings on earth, deserving the most severe punishments. Likewise, he condemned as absolute wickedness necromancy and ceremonies aimed at coercing evil spirits: all conjurations were against God and contrary to his Word. Those who, by means of conjurations, forced the spirits to do their bidding were, he thought, comparable to thieves and murderers whose crimes deserved the noose. Condemning those who did such things was, however, not a denial of the utility of hidden mysteries. On the contrary, Paracelsus' universe – with its ideas of powers emanating from the heavens and spiritual beings all around – proclaimed the practical value and efficacy of the magical arts that established bonds of sympathy between different parts of creation.

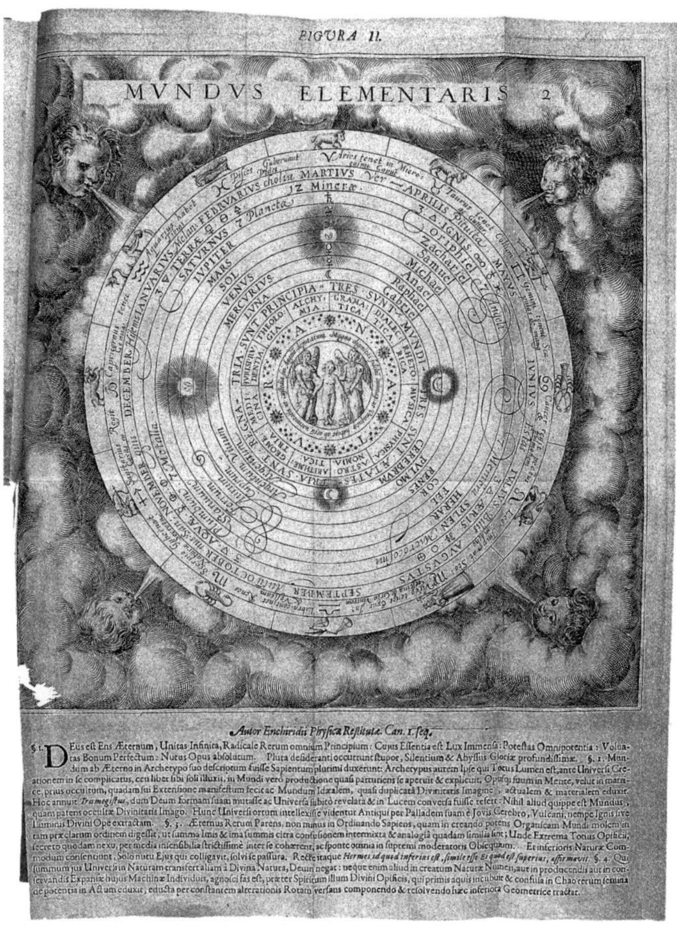

True magic, as opposed to *Zauberei* (the illegitimate and diabolical sort), brought the powers of the heavens within the grasp of the human being. It was the art by which one could come to know how to bring celestial powers into stones, herbs and even words. It taught how to change one thing into another and how to recognize what was supernatural in the

19 The powers of the heavens embedded in the elementary world, from *Musaeum hermeticum reformatum et amplificatum* (1678), a collection of alchemical tracts.

order of nature. The true *magus* always operated in a way that fulfilled the work of God, and in this way, combined what was natural with what was holy. Becoming a magician was, in this way, a divine calling, an art that could not be learned from books but to which one was born. It is probably for this reason that there is very little to be found in Paracelsus' writings concerning the actual practice of magic, and scholars of his work struggle over which writings ascribed to him concerning occult philosophy and magic were, indeed, written by him. One book especially, the *Archidoxis magica* (Archidoxes of Magic), presents just such a problem. It was first pulled together as a volume in the late sixteenth century and as such, could not have been designed by the hand of Paracelsus himself. Even so, the book seems largely representative of Paracelsus' own judgements and ideas, and it may have been constructed, at least in part, from his original writings. Many would have agreed with the general view it expressed: just as God made the physician to recognize the powers contained in animals, plants and minerals – that is, what made them useful for making medicines – God appointed the *magus* to recognize the celestial powers contained in the objects of nature and to bring those powers into the service of the human being. The *magus* thus could discern nature's hidden virtues and powers and knew how to collect and direct those powers to produce changes and wonders. Those powers excited things; they made things happen.

Among the most interesting occult practices described in the *Archidoxis* and other writings attributed to Paracelsus were those that referred to the powers contained in words and characters (secret symbols), as well as in images. Words worked on the imagination, and Paracelsus aligned the imaginative power, and the powers contained in words and names, with the forces of nature. Those powers were available to the true *magus*, but witches and necromancers knew how to make use of them as well – and they would do so, often by means of conjurations and incantations, to serve their own ends. After all, God had endowed the Devil with art and had made him highly learned in the light of nature. Thus, ironically, human beings needed to know what the Devil knew. God was, after all, the author of all true knowledge, and that included the kind of knowledge that the Devil misapplied. Moreover, just because a certain kind of knowledge involving spirits and spiritual forces seemed incredible and outside the natural norm, it did not mean that it was automatically sorcery. Thinking so could not be more delightful to the Devil. 'We should not accord such an honor to the devil,' he writes, 'For what could possibly please him more, even with all his idolatry, than receiving such praise as when we say that he [rather than God] is the one who has done this'? Even matters seemingly incomprehensible to the learned were not necessarily diabolical. As he writes, 'if we were to have no experience of such things, we would not know what God is. Would that be a proper state of affairs for the human being: to know nothing?'[22] Anyone who would advise such a thing would indeed be a sorcerer himself.

The Devil was clever. He had presented himself, Paracelsus argued, as the inventor of *magica* in order that no one who wanted to be close to God would practise it. Thus he had played an enormous trick on mankind. But the true Christian could see through the ruse, he said, and knew that it was his

Christian duty to learn the magical art: 'If we can learn from the devil his entire art, we should do so, thereby making use of the [magical] art and leaving the devil alone.'[23] This was the way to recognize God's mysteries as they existed in all sorts of created things. Thus there was no reason to hold the art of magic in contempt since, by doing so, one limited the human ability to cure and protect humankind, especially from illnesses that were themselves caused by sorcery. One needed to beat the Devil at his own game, and nature possessed an abundance of invisible spirits to help one do so. Thus, he says,

> if the visible body is capable of crafting itself a set of armor for [protection against] blows and stabbing beneath which the visible and invisible body are likewise protected, then in cases of dire need the invisible body might also fashion for itself an invisible armor in order to protect and preserve the invisible body, and with it the visible one as well.[24]

Great are the virtues of nature; and all of them, all the invisible powers of the universe, were condensed in the small world of the human being. According to Paracelsus, one of those powers, the power of life itself, survived even when the visible body was dead. If extracted, he reasoned, it could be used as the base of a powerful medicament. We have entered here into one of the most curious chambers of Paracelsus' medical mansion, the realm of an invisible power called *mumia* (literally 'mummy'). This is not the literal sort that we encountered earlier, but a special Paracelsian variety. Scholars in the late Renaissance knew about *mumia* from ancient Greek and Arabic sources. Usually it referred to a medicine extracted from bodies that had been embalmed with certain ingredients such as aloes, myrrh or asphalt (bitumen). It could also generally refer to a body's desiccated remains. Paracelsus referred to *mumia* in several ways: it could be a balsam extracted from commonplace materials; or it could equally become endowed with cosmic significance, as a celestial life- and health-giving spirit that connected the body to the cosmos and continued in the body even after death. In the same way that the visible body sees and speaks though nobody can see sight or speech, Paracelsus argued, the physical body always retained an invisible body or *mumia* of life itself. When the physical body died, the *mumia*, the connection to the life of the cosmos, was still there. 'The body in the grave,' Paracelsus notes, 'retains the nature of the planets and stars, with their nature and powers that never come to an end [in acting] upon us.'[25]

Near the end of his little book concerning invisible diseases, Paracelsus drew a parallel between the action of *mumia* and what the Sun does when it shines through glass, or what fire does when its heat passes through an oven. In both cases, a body – the Sun or the fire – remains in one place but sends its powers far away from itself. In the human body, that power was a magnetic mumial spirit, and it revealed itself in wondrous ways. For example, Paracelsus writes,

> Let's say someone is murdered. Much later it comes about that the murderer is standing near this body and it bleeds . . . [This is] an indication that our blood cries out to God and to the authorities for revenge.[26]

The connection is by means of sympathies and the celestial powers existing in the blood that reach across space. By such means, some followers of Paracelsus thought that one could treat a wound by applying a salve that included the victim's blood to the weapon rather than the wound itself. Our modern sensibilities may cause us to chuckle at this, but the weapon salve was no joke, and the medicament had its supporters even among those who rejected in general Paracelsus' medical and philosophical opinions.

Others inspired by Paracelsus' thinking, such as the German physicians Oswald Croll (1563–1609) and Andreas Tentzel (*fl.* 1625), helped push ideas about *mumia* yet further. To prepare the mumial spirit as a medicament, they reasoned, it was important to find the right body. A criminal who had been strangled or hanged was preferable to others. In such cases, *mumia* would be concentrated in the head and could be easily scraped off with the matter coating the inside of the skull. In a book which claimed to have been abstracted from the works of Paracelsus, but which only appeared in English much later, Tentzel commented that,

> if Physicians . . . understood the right use of this Mumie or [knew] what it is good for, not any Malefactors would be left three daies on the Gallowes, or continue on the Wheel, from being stolen away; for they [physicians] would run any hazard for procuring of these Bodies.[27]

What was natural and what was supernatural, what was of God and what was not, were real concerns to Paracelsus and his followers because the things of nature and those beyond were interwoven in daily experience. Some, such as the Italian philosopher Giovanni Francesco Pico della Mirandola (1469–1533) tried to discrimate between natural and demonic magic by claiming that natural magic worked automatically while demonic magic worked only by constraint. But Paracelsus knew that the constraint of nature was essential to learning about her properties and powers. Magic, in this sense, signified the highest perfection of natural wisdom. While astonishing at first, natural magic, properly understood, became quite ordinary.

Nonetheless, in Paracelsus' thinking, that which was essential to being and life – namely, a body's fifth essence, that impure form of the stuff of the universe, midway between soul and body – could not be defined by the logic of schools or weighed out on the scales. Paracelsian medicine was always tied to the heavens, and Paracelsus himself was known to many through the astrological and prophetic writings that were published during his lifetime. Later, in the 1560s, these works came together in a major collection called *Astronomica et astrologica* (1567), in which were described the intimate connections between the astral and the divine. The study of astronomy – which, for Paracelsus meant the study of astral spirits – was thus, in fact, a form of natural theology. Like the higher theology, it brought the investigator closer to a knowledge of God by means of belief in the supernatural. The small world of the human being contained the great world in itself; and the astronomer, as natural theologian, understood the relationship between the divine and the workings of the *machina mundi* within the human microcosm.

When Paracelsus died in 1541, most of the writings that would be ascribed to him in the years to come were as yet unpublished. Soon individual texts, edited and published in both Latin and German, began to appear, and between 1589 and 1591 a ten-volume collection of Paracelsus' writings was made available, edited and published by a physician named Johann Huser (1545–c. 1600). At the beginning of the collection, Huser distinguished which writings he had come by that were in Paracelsus' own hand (autograph manuscripts) and which had come to him as copies from other sources. One of the major sources for manuscripts was a collector and friend, a doctor living in Silesia named Johannes Scultetus Montanus (1531–1604). Paracelsus scholars ever since have argued about which texts are genuine and which are not, or which may have been altered in the process of transmission. Nevertheless, on the basis of those ten edited volumes, Paracelsus' reputation as an alchemist, mystic, physician, theologian and/or magician began to take shape. The followers of Paracelsus have each distinguished themselves on the basis of what they chose to keep or reject from those writings. Some were moved by mystical ideas, others preferred practical chemistry. Some underscored the relevance of a holistic approach to treating the sick, eschewing a strictly mechanical view to the body. Paracelsus lived on in the imagination, and the invention of Paracelsus in the centuries that followed is itself one of the most interesting aspects of the story of Paracelsus.

SEVEN

Inventing Paracelsus: The Use and Abuse of a Renaissance Life

It could be said that, in the most technical sense, historians do not actually study 'the past'. This may sound absurd to some, but the thing we call 'the past' does not exist as an object with which we can directly engage. We cannot put it under a microscope, observe it and record what we see – but this is not to say that we cannot know anything about it. In discussing 'the past', what we really study are the leftovers from a time before our own, its residual texts and writings, its artefacts, its material and physical remains. It is worth reminding ourselves of this because historical accounts are, in many ways, inventions, creations of the present based upon interpretations of that residual evidence. As new evidence comes to light, what we know may change. Likewise, as older evidence once thought genuine is shown to be fictitious or untrustworthy, our judgements may change accordingly. What makes this especially important in the case of Paracelsus is that our residual evidence is, from the very beginning, full of holes. Worse still, it has often been tampered with.

As mentioned earlier, very few of the texts ascribed to Paracelsus were actually published during his lifetime. When manuscripts did come to light after his death, those who edited and published his works necessarily made judgements about what was genuine. At times, these editorial judgements extended to what they thought Paracelsus meant to say, and as a result, publishers sometimes made insertions of their own. This leaves us with several problems and some important questions: which texts ascribed to Paracelsus are actually written by him and which are not? Can we believe everything he says about himself regardless of whether it is him saying it? How much of what he writes concerning his own life and wanderings can be supported by other evidence? And how much of what has been written about Paracelsus in the intervening years should we trust? Like many other historical figures, the legacy and image of Paracelsus has been used and abused. He has been made into a mystical sage, a literary figure, a Romantic hero, a subject of psychoanalysis and a symbol of politico-cultural ideology. For example, when commenting on a collection of texts not published until the mid-twentieth century, the Paracelsus scholar Walter Pagel (1898–1983) thought it necessary to insist that 'Paracelsus . . . was not a Nazi.'[1] But why would he feel it necessary to do so?

We know far more about the life and work of Paracelsus than ever before. Good studies exist, and well-informed and cautious Paracelsian scholars do not simply fabricate facts. Nevertheless, in terms of the ways in which the life and work of Paracelsus have been interpreted and their relevance assessed, we are forever dealing with the Paracelsus of the imagination, the Paracelsus invented for purposes of personal and cultural utility. Paracelsus engaged his own world and broke its rules. Each subsequent age, however, is further removed from that world, and in reappraising his significance, each gets the Paracelsus it wants.

For a while, at the end of the sixteenth century and well into the century following, his status was that of a medical prophet, a Renaissance figure who inspired new practices in medicine and aroused the interests of mystical theologians. The practical side of his medical ideas in particular – understanding the body chemically and fashioning chemical medicines to cure chemical diseases – served to create a new group of so-called 'chemical physicians', or *iatrochemists*. Then, silence followed. The eighteenth century, the age of reason and Enlightenment, was, for the most part, embarrassed by mysticism and magic and placed Paracelsus in the company of charlatans, quacks and fools. Nevertheless, in some circles – not least the group around the Swedish philosopher, theologian and mystic Emanuel Swedenborg (1688–1772), who sought out ways in which spirit and matter were joined in nature (and who claimed to be able to talk to angels and demons while visiting heaven and hell) – Paracelsus held a respected place, not as a physician but as a mystical forerunner. Traditions of occultism and esotericism from Rosicrucians and Cabalists to Theosophists also claimed Paracelsus as a prominent predecessor.[2] In one way, however, even the Enlightenment recognized something of a continuing Paracelsian influence in the world of medicine, although it is one that Paracelsus himself would hardly have expected. The German writer, dramatist and philosopher Gotthold Lessing (1729–1781) credited him as the actual discoverer of the so-called 'magnetic cure' made popular during the period by the much-travelled Viennese physician Franz Mesmer (1734–1815).

The cultural revival of Paracelsus has much to do with a literary, artistic and philosophical movement that began in the eighteenth century and carried on well into the nineteenth: Romanticism. One of the greatest authors in German literature, Johann Wolfgang von Goethe (1749–1832), stood at the forefront of this renaissance. Goethe knew and studied the works of Paracelsus, even though the opportunities to do so were few at the time. One of his best-known characters, the figure of Faust – the alchemist–physician whose yearning for knowledge and passion for nature leads to a pact with the Devil – is generally thought to be influenced by the image of Paracelsus. The soul of Goethe's Faust is certainly twisted, but in the end, he does not lose it. Perhaps echoing a feeling for Paracelsus, in Part II of Goethe's version Faust is saved at the last minute by angels who declare, 'Wer immer strebend sich bemueht, Den koennen wir erloesen' (he who endeavours, always striving, he is one we can redeem).

It is hard to define the Romantic movement in a way that suits all occasions. This is because what gets called Romanticism is more of a mood than a doctrine – and moods change. Nevertheless, some characteristics seem more or less shared by its proponents, among them a preference for the kind of subjective insight that gives weight to individual discernment, inspiration and emotion when coming to grips with the experience of nature and the world. In this regard, Paracelsus' ideas are easily compatible with the temper of Romantic authors, especially the German ones. Like Paracelsus, they were drifters, driven by wanderlust but always yearning for home. They, too, broke through learned limits that defined what was certain; and they wished to be absorbed by nature, or at least to find transcendence in being awed by her powers. No wonder that Paracelsian notions like the analogy of the micro- and macrocosm, a physical world packed with spirits and the notion of the human being as corporeal, astral and divine, fascinated and charmed these thinkers and writers.

Though many of the German Romantic authors may be relatively unknown to English readers, a few examples will be useful. One of the earliest is a man who died very young, before he reached the age of 29. His name was Friedrich von Hardenberg, but he is best known by his pen name, Novalis (1772–1801). 'Philosophy', he wrote, 'is actually homesickness, [one is] driven to be everywhere in order to be at home.'[3] Paracelsus would have felt that deeply, and that shared feeling may be one of the reasons why Novalis planned to write a novel about Paracelsus. Of course, we cannot know for sure what that novel would have looked like: death intruded before he really got started on it; and, in any case, given the numerous traditions that influenced his thinking, it is difficult to discern which of Novalis' ideas were directly derived from Paracelsus. Nevertheless, from written fragments left behind that articulate various ideas around poetry, medicine, physics and magic, there is good indication of the central role played by Paracelsus in the dreamy yet practical world Novalis intended to fashion in writing. Of particular significance was what he called Paracelsus' 'theological physics' – the ideas that 'everything visible clings to the invisible' and that the human being was a microcosm of the universe. 'We dream of travelling through the universe,' Novalis wrote, '[but] is the universe not in us?'[4] Just as Paracelsus' spirits were connected to the elements, so magic ran through the physics of what was thought concrete. 'The world', Novalis asserted, is 'made living by me. It is . . . one with me.'[5] Thus 'the physical magus knows how to animate nature and, like his own body, attend to it at will.'[6] To Novalis and Paracelsus alike, the human being was, by nature, a magus possessing 'a power similar to the stars, by means of which he or she becomes as powerful as the heavens'.[7]

In many ways, it was through Novalis that Paracelsus came to influence the Romantic era, mixing poetry with science and producing poetic magic as a result – 'cultural chemistry' resulting in philosophical magic. The chemist knows, he wrote, 'that by means of a genuine mixture [of two things] a third comes into being that is both like and more than the [former] two.'[8] Nature and art produced the *magus*, nature's way of knowing itself and making new things. 'Everything is magic or nothing.'[9] Human beings had simply ignored how magical they were, Novalis reasoned:

> The greatest magician would be the one who [along with other things,] could so enchant himself that to him the results of his [own] wizardry would seem like alien, self-empowered appearances. Could that not be the case with us?[10]

Magic was making, and to make something was to know it. The poet and the magus alike did that; thus, for Novalis, Paracelsus was a poetic magus.

Other German Romantics rediscovered Paracelsus, following their own agendas, often combining anecdotes, fairy tales and history to arouse poetic feelings. To Novalis's close friend Friedrich Schlegel (1772–1829), Paracelsus counted as both a mystic and modern philosopher, but one not without blemishes – not least his secretiveness and charlatanism. Others took up Paracelsus' elementary spirits, incorporating his world of nymphs and sprites into a subcategory of Romantic literature. Among them were the storyteller E.T.A. Hoffmann (1776–1822), Ludwig Tieck (1773–1853), Friedrich de la Motte Fouqué (1777–1843) and Ludwig Achim von Arnim (1781–1831). Others still began to treat Paracelsus himself as a historical personality, a heroic rebel, misunderstood and maligned by the world around him. In the image they created of Paracelsus, myth and legend often got the better of history as the Romantic imagination found in him a font of mystical emotion and enigmatic wonder.[11]

Over time, artistic depictions of Paracelsus also changed.[12] Art historians and Paracelsus scholars count around two hundred illustrations that attempt to portray him, yet only a few of these were actually made during his lifetime. The best-known, and perhaps the most realistic, since produced during his lifetime, are two images made by an anonymous artist in the years 1538 and 1540, at the time that Paracelsus was preparing his *Seven Defences*. These may have been intended for the planned publication of his *Carinthian Writings* or could have been intended for printing as broadsides (a way of publicly posting ideas on a single sheet of paper, similar to a poster or newspaper page). Both portraits bear the iconic caption 'Alterius non sit qui suus esse potest', but the later image, which appeared the year before his death, depicts a man on whom life has evidently taken its toll. Both images were of Paracelsus when older and formed the basis for other images to follow – printed from carved woodblocks or etched

copperplates – which accompanied many of Paracelsus' texts when they were first published in the 1560s. They also stand as the source for a number of images made at the end of the sixteenth century that depict Paracelsus in the company of other notable figures, including physicians, judges, theologians and politicians. One of the most important images (illus. 20) that allied Paracelsus with such notables was made by a copperplate engraver from the Netherlands (who also owned

20 Image of Paracelsus after Theodor de Bry, from Jean-Jacques Boissard, *Icones et effigies* (1645).

a bookstore in Frankfurt) named Theodor de Bry (1528–1598). Images of Paracelsus painted in oils also begin to appear at the end of the sixteenth and beginning of the seventeenth centuries, and they too refer back to the elderly figure of the two earliest depictions.

21 Copy of the lost portrait of Paracelsus by Quentin Matsys (*c.* 1465–1530).

Other images, however, attempted to portray a much younger Paracelsus, and in this regard, there can be no sense of an actual likeness. One, claiming to be a portrayal of Paracelsus aged 24, may have been modelled on a self-portrait by a student of Rembrandt named Ferdinand Bol (1616–1680). Another, showing a chubbier Paracelsus, has a more definite origin, now surviving only as a copy of the lost original painted by a well-known artist from Antwerp named Quentin Matsys (Quinten Massys, 1466–1530) (illus. 21). The plump Paracelsus survived also in a copy of the copy of Metsys's painting made by Peter Paul Rubens (1577–1640), an artist famed for depicting fleshy figures (albeit more often of nude women). Rubens's depiction inspired others, and plump Paracelsus caught on as the model of choice for numerous engravers and painters well into the eighteenth century.

Some images thought to be portraits of Paracelsus turn out to be no such thing. For a long time a piece believed to be a preliminary drawing for a painting that was to be called 'Paracelsus' was attributed to Hans Holbein the Younger, one of the greatest portraitists of the sixteenth century. The image was considered a creditable early depiction of the young and confident physician, but this claim transpired to be completely unfounded. The work is most likely by an unknown artist of the mid-seventeenth century. Today the picture, held at the Basel Art Museum, is referred to only as *Young Man with a Slouch Hat*. Another image of Paracelsus, this one created by a Parisian painter and engraver named François Chauveau (1613–1676) and later used on the title page of a 1658 Swiss edition of his collected works, depicted him as a thin, middle-aged figure with a beard, large hands and curly

hair (illus. 22). Preempting any doubts, Chauveau claimed that the figure was based on a picture made by the Venetian artist Tintoretto (1519–1594), who, he said, made the image from life. At best, this stretches credulity, since the possible date of any sort of likely opportunity for Paracelsus and the Venetian artist to have met is at least a couple of years before the artist was born. Chauveau was inventing a Paracelsus no one would have recognized, yet that image – like the plump Paracelsus created by Metsys and copied by Rubens – was copied by others, becoming another means for later generations to make his acquaintance.

22 Image of Paracelsus in the tradition of François Chauveau, from *Paracelsus* by Robert Browning (1899).

23 Portrait of Paracelsus burning the books of the fathers of medicine, by Ernest Board (1877–1934), commissioned by Henry Wellcome, oil on canvas.

The Romantics inherited these images and imaginings of Paracelsus. Since depicting feeling was more important than claims to likeness, imagination and invention clearly had an advantage. What these artists wanted were representations that could relate moments of personal striving, wonder and statements of mystical power – something, anything, that could create the staged consciousness of an inner being. The result could be theatrical, as in a work by the Salzburg portrait painter Sebastian Stief (1811–1889) that depicts a robed Paracelsus gazing at a distilled elixir, a hero–creator producing a medicament for the benefit of humanity. Another painting, by the Austrian painter Hans Makart (1840–1884), shows Paracelsus the magician and alchemist, asleep in a chair in a darkened room. A servant, humble, reverent and awed, draws near, filling the scene with sentiments of curiosity, admiration and the trepidation of wonder. When later the pharmaceutical entrepreneur and collector of medical artefacts Henry Wellcome (1853–1936) wanted to depict great moments in the history of medicine, the image of Paracelsus turned theatrically into a combination of Martin Luther's defiance and a sort of medical Moses destroying another sort of sacred calf (illus. 23).

Romantic philosophy, too, was touched by the rekindling interest in Paracelsus. This was especially the case in the tradition of what is called Romantic nature philosophy, the holistic attempt to comprehend the world as a dynamic, living structure in which spirit, matter, self-consciousness and time itself interrelated as part of the being of nature. Although part of a larger philosophical setting that connects to the thinking of, among others, the influential German philosopher Immanuel

Kant (1724–1804), nature philosophy acquired its special speculative characteristics – and its place in Romantic medicine – from a German scholar named Friedrich Wilhelm Joseph Schelling (1775–1854). Schelling placed special emphasis on a continuity between organic and inorganic nature, arguing for a unity of all the forces of nature and against simple mechanical explanations. In particular, he joined the consciousness of the self to the discovery of the external world, arguing in one of his first major publications, *Ideas for a Philosophy of Nature* (1797), that

> With the first consciousness of the external world, the consciousness of myself is also there, and also the other way around, in the first moment of my consciousness, the actual world opens itself up before me. The belief in the reality outside me arises and grows with the belief in myself; one is as necessary as the other.[13]

Schelling was careful not to claim that it is self-consciousness that produces the external world, believing that would be an especially dangerous and radically subjective philosophy to uphold. Nevertheless, self-consciousness was integrated into nature, he thought, as part of the process of nature's own evolution. Where Paracelsus considered human beings to be nature's way of knowing herself, Schelling viewed nature as producing, over time, human self-consciousness. Aware that mind and matter were intertwined, in later life Schelling began to look to the occult – including such things as animal magnetism, dreams and psychic phenomena – as ways of understanding the link.

Those who represented Romantic nature philosophy and Romantic medicine may have shared a world view in which Paracelsus would have felt, for the most part, at home, but there is very little direct reference to his theories and practices in that later philosophical and medical writing. Most knew of the historical figure of Paracelsus through general references in lexicons and encyclopaedias where he was cast into the company of charlatans or of great thinkers, or sometimes both.

While some scoffed, others openly praised Paracelsus. An article on the 'History and Present State of Chemical Science' that appeared in the *Edinburgh Review* in October 1829 remarked upon Paracelsus' deep knowledge of nature, acknowledging that since Paracelsus

> was a zealous cultivator of Chemistry, and extolled chemical medicines to the skies, he threw a lustre upon the science of which it was before destitute . . . The invectives of Paracelsus against Galen and Avicenna . . . were probably necessary to rouse the attention of mankind, and to induce medical men to abandon the jargon of the schools . . . If we compare the formulae of Paracelsus with those of Boyle, published a century and a half later, we will not have much to boast of the superiority of the nostrums of our own countryman, above those of the Basil professor.[14]

Someone who may have read that article, either when it was published or not long after, was a young English poet who was, at this time, just beginning to make a literary name for himself: Robert Browning (1812–1889).[15]

Influenced by a French friend, Browning made Paracelsus the focus of a play that was meant to be read rather than acted. The poem–drama was called, fittingly enough, *Paracelsus* (1835), and in it Browning presented not so much a historical character as a character of the imagination, representing his own subjective view of the relation between learning, love and moral progress.[16] In Browning's invention, Paracelsus feels chosen by God to do great things, indeed to 'comprehend the works of God, and God himself, and all God's intercourse with the human mind'.[17] His plan is to gather 'the sacred knowledge, here and there dispersed About the World, long lost or never found'.[18] Paracelsus vows to 'learn how to set free the soul alike in all, discovering the true laws by which the flesh accloys the spirit', and thus to 'become a star to men for ever'.[19] Browning's character wants to be a superstar, but he does not love those for whom he wishes to be a hero. It does not take long for him to feel that something is missing in his search for knowledge: his soul is empty; he has sought knowledge at the expense of love. Gradually, he learns that love and knowledge must exist together. Knowledge, this Paracelsus comes to understand, emerges through love (which, as we have seen, was also a view held by the real Paracelsus), while wisdom and expertise become the ways in which love enters the world. For all its attention to love and leaning, there is also a social–critical side to this unacted drama. As Browning has Paracelsus say,

> And men seem made, though not as I believed, For something better than these times produce. Witness

> these gangs of peasants . . . whom Münzer leads, and whom the duke, the landgrave, and the elector will calm in blood![20]

Paracelsus may have thought himself to be God's gift to humanity, 'like some knight traversing a wilderness' who 'may chance to free a tribe of desert-people from their dragon-foe' – so a saviour right enough, but one aloof and disconnected from the rescued.[21] By the close of Browning's work, the tone has changed. Human beings don't need a saviour, it transpires, at least not one of this sort. They can do things for themselves, bring about a better world through the wrenching, sometimes squalid and heartbreaking development of the human spirit. And so Paracelsus dies realizing his double error. He learnt to love another and thought that was enough. But he never learned to love mankind.

> I stood at first where all aspire at last
> To stand: the secret of the world was mine.
> I knew, I felt . . .
> . . . what God is, what we are,
> What life is . . .
> Yet constituted thus, and thus endowed,
> I failed: I gazed on power till I grew blind.
> Power; I could not take my eyes from that . . .
> . . . I learned my own deep error; love's undoing
> Taught me the worth of love in man's estate . . .
> . . .
> I learned this, and supposed the whole was learned:
> And thus, when men received with stupid wonder

My first revealings, [and] would have worshipped me,
. . . I despised and loathed their proffered praise –
. . . and I hated them . . .
. . . In my own heart love had not been made wise
To trace love's faint beginnings in mankind,
To know even hate is but a mask of love's,
To see a good in evil, and a hope
In ill success; to sympathize, be proud
Of their half-reasons, faint aspirings, dim
Struggles for truth . . .
. . .
All this I knew not, and I failed.[22]

Humanity, it seems, has no need of magicians nor metaphysics. It just needs to keep trying. At the last, Browning's Paracelsus appears as both a warning and a promise. 'Let men / Regard me', he says, 'Who loved too rashly; and shape "forth" a third / And better-tempered spirit, warned by both.'[23] Included in rather than separated from an evolving and combative human spirit, Paracelsus' own ideas, while subject to transient criticism and disdain, secure a place in futurity. His dying words are both realistic and confident:

. . . I have done well, though not all well.
As yet man cannot do without contempt;
'Tis for their good, and therefore fit awhile
That they reject the weak, and scorn the false,
Rather than praise the strong and true, in me:
But after, they will know me. If I stoop
Into a dark tremendous sea of cloud,

> It is but for a time . . .
> . . . [I] will pierce the gloom: I shall emerge one day.[24]

Browning's *Paracelsus* was really a poem borrowing the form of a play; it would not be until 1 March 1899 that Paracelsus would actually step onto the stage. The venue was the Burgtheater in Vienna. The play, simply called *Paracelsus*, was written by the Austrian physician, author and playwright Arthur Schnitzler (1862–1931).[25] Schnitzler's Vienna was the world of sexuality and psychoanalysis, characterized most prominently by the art of Gustav Klimt and the writings of Sigmund Freud. The once hidden world of the unconscious (a word first used by the nature philosopher Schelling) was everywhere on display. One of Schnitzler's plays, *Reigen* (made into a French language film in 1950 and translated as *La Ronde*), assembles characters before and after having sex. Freud was enthusiastic about it and observed that Schnitzler had really captured the connections between sexuality, repression and the unconscious. In a letter written to the author on the occasion of his sixtieth birthday, Freud made what he called an intimate confession:

> [I have been] struggling with the question of why I have never, in all these years, made any effort to meet you and to talk with you . . . I think I have avoided you out of a kind of fear of finding my own double . . . [because] when I read one of your beautiful works I seem to encounter again and again, behind the poetic fiction, the presumptions, interests, and conclusions so well known to me from my own

> thoughts . . . I have thus gained the impression that you have learned through intuition – although actually as a result of sensitive introspection – everything that I have had to unearth by laborious work on other persons.[26]

Given the context, it is not surprising that Schnitzler's *Paracelsus* unfolds within the world of dreams and their meaning.[27] Paracelsus, the outsider, is invited into the ordered, middle-class home of the bourgeois weaponsmith Cyprian. 'This is my house, as it was my father's, and my ancestors' for three hundred years,' Cyprian explains. His wife, Justina, is a woman from Paracelsus' past, a woman he had formerly loved. In a playful act of hypnosis ('Are you afraid of memories? One can do no better to take away what makes you shudder than if one reawakens them to life') she enters the world of the unconscious. What Cyprian hears thereafter shocks him, as Justina confesses something he did not wish to know. 'Know only Justina as she is,' Paracelsus advises, 'innocent and yet guilty . . . chaste yet unchaste, carrying, in the senses, the remembrance of wild embers'.[28] In the end, enlightenment follows commotion, and Cyprian observes that 'A windstorm came that for a moment tore open the gates of our soul, and we took a quick glance . . . It was a game, yet I found its meaning.'[29] Paracelsus, he concedes, 'brought truth into this house of lies'.[30] The truth for Schnitzler, however, lay somewhere else, in a kind of relativity that made all else fade away except for the moment. 'It was a game,' he has Paracelsus say,

> What else should it be? What is not a game that we do on earth, and it seemed yet to be so great and deep . . . Dream and wakefulness, truth and lies shove into one another. Certainty is nowhere. We know nothing of others, nothing of ourselves. We're always just playing; you're savvy if you know that.[31]

Schnitzler's plays and other writings were not, however, considered a game by the new order which rose in 1930s Germany – namely, the National Socialist Party of Adolf Hitler. The Nazis banned Schnitzler's works, branding them 'Jewish filth', and most likely, his writings were among the estimated 25,000 books tossed into the flames outside Berlin's celebrated opera house (today Bebelplatz) on 10 May 1933 when the German Student Union organized 'an action against the un-German spirit'. But while Schnitzler's creations may have gone up in smoke, the works of Paracelsus gained increasing esteem. Paracelsus was once again reinvented, this time as an icon of hyper-Germanness, a nationalist hero who struggled against savage attacks from all sides for the good of the *Volk*. He became a figure close to nature, mystically connected to natural forces and rooted, by way of language and peasant culture, in German blood and soil (*Blut und Boden*). The German Society for the History of Medicine and Natural Sciences (founded in 1901) had also rediscovered Paracelsus, and, although there is certainly no direct link, the effort to produce the first complete collection of Paracelsus' writings since the sixteenth century – a major undertaking of fourteen volumes edited and published between 1929 and 1938 by the physician and historian Karl Sudhoff (1853–1938) – helped provide the academic framework for the Nazi fantasy. Sudhoff himself became a member of the National Socialist Party in 1933 at the age of eighty.

In literature, too, Paracelsus found himself in the spotlight. Shaping his popular image was a romantic–nationalist trilogy published between 1917 and 1926 by the German-Austrian novelist, playwright and philosopher Erwin Guido Kolbenheyer (1878–1962). The characters of different peoples [*Völker*], Kolbenheyer thought, were essentially determined by biology. The German people had, in this regard, a special destiny and between 1933 and 1944 he publicly supported the National Socialists, joining the Nazi Party in 1940. Paracelsus, in Kolbenheyer's invention, mirrored the genius of the German people, and this view now became the stuff of Nazi propaganda. Further, three plays by another Austrian, Martha Sills-Fuchs (1896–?), made Paracelsus a central character, and he is clearly portrayed as a precursor of Nazi ideology, tying what is pure in nature to racism and anti-Semitism. Commenting on Kolbenheyer's trilogy (the third part of which is forebodingly titled *Paracelsus' Third Reich*) in a book called *Paracelsus and Us* (1941), Sills-Fuchs drew attention to the novel's final words: *Ecce ingenium teutonicum* (Behold the Teutonic genius). Taking up the theme, she writes,

> Behold the German soul! Just like this life, this struggle, creativity, and experience, this looking upward and these fateful steps of Paracelsus, this is what the German individual can be, this is the prepared form of his being, here is the soul of a people raised up so as to be [the model for] a Type of person . . . Especially

> today . . . it is necessary to remember once again those men of our blood who lived before us a true German life . . . A magical power, the primal force of life itself, long remarked upon by Paracelsus, will thrust mankind onto the single path of its future: to the display of the unity of God, man, and nature.[32]

Five books were published about Paracelsus in the German-speaking world in 1941 alone, all of them supremely nationalistic in flavour. One, a historical novel called *König der Ärzte* (King of Physicians) by Pert Peternell, inspired a motion picture. The director was the respected film-maker Georg W. Pabst (1885–1967), whose films span the years 1923 to 1956.[33] In the 1920s and '30s Pabst steadfastly supported the type of social revolution inspired by Karl Marx, and followed other film-makers in graphically depicting the agonies of the First World War in his 1930 film *Westfront 1918*. After living in France and the United States, he found himself in Austria at the time of the German invasion of Poland and found it difficult to leave thereafter. As a film-maker residing in Nazi Germany, the Nazi authorities requisitioned Pabst's talents to make films for purposes of general entertainment. Pabst's critics suspect collaboration even though he refused to take part in making explicit Nazi propaganda. Nevertheless, Paracelsus was a hot ticket and the film that Pabst created, *Paracelsus* (1943) – from a script written by Kurt Heuser and starring Werner Kraus – was both a historical drama and a filmic portrait of a 'great man'. What it was not, at least in any overt sort of way, was hysterical or bombastic Nazi puffery. Some are adamant that it was a National Socialist film, but if it was, it projected most prominently the socialist side of National Socialism. While mysticism and adversity fill the frames, the story relates to Paracelsus' love of the poor and his intense caring for those abandoned by regular medicine during a time of plague.

The year 1941 also saw plans for a International Paracelsus Conference, an assembly of the best Paracelsus scholars from across the globe. Hitler himself might appear, the conference planners thought, and certainly the Nazi ideologue Alfred Rosenberg (1893–1946) must be invited. The *Reichsminister* for science and education, Bernard Rust (1883–1945), was also reserved a seat, as were Joseph Goebbels (1897–1945) and the *Reichsgesundheitsführer* (Reich Health Leader) Leonardo Conti (1900–1945). As described by historian and Salzburg archivist Peter Kramml, the event was to take place in Salzburg from 20 to 28 September 1941.[34] No fewer than 50,000 people were expected. A monument was to be erected and there would be a multimedia exhibition of pictures, portraits, documents and books in the Great Hall of the University, with dioramas prepared by the German Propaganda Atelier in Berlin illustrating important moments in the hero–physician's life. The ticket price for the event was estimated at 380,000 Reichmarks. The Mayor of Salzburg was certain that the war would be over before the conference opened. The organizers timetabled lectures by well-known researchers, although controversy arose as to whether the novelist Kolbenheyer was academic and scientific enough to take the place of Karl Sudhoff, who had died several years earlier. Such were the plans. By June 1941, however, the situation had dramatically changed. The Nazi invasion of Russia (Operation Barbarossa) began on 22 June, and the international mega-event was cancelled.

But a smaller affair now came into view. This would take place between 23 and 25 September, with entry costing a mere 35,000 Reichsmarks. The new plans jettisoned the more scholarly side of the conference but left the ideology in place. *Reichsminister* for the interior Wilhelm Frick (1877–1946) and Leonardo Conti were the main speakers. Frick turned Paracelsus into an ideological Jew hater. Paracelsus, he said, wanted nothing to do with Jews, alien blood or foreign mentalities, and rejected all those inferior in body and mind. Of the world that Paracelsus sought, he proclaimed, 'that [world] shall and will be realized in the medical service of the Third Reich'.[35] Conti, for his part, also emphasized Paracelsus' disdain of Jews and praised his conservative views on marriage and producing children. It was not possible, of course, for anyone to be a National Socialist in the sixteenth century, but, Conti added, 'whoever knows the worth of blood and of his people, whoever is a fighter and great personality . . . he stands close to us and to our view of the world.'[36] Paracelsus was a true National Socialist, they claimed, if not in life, then in his soul.

All that is behind us now, but who knows what new invention awaits. These days, if you discount its appearance in occult contexts and rock 'n' roll, the image of Paracelsus is, by and large, constructed on sound scholarship that links his ideas both to the history of science and medicine and to the religious and spiritual world of the Reformation. On the basis of those studies which include the preparation of a new and more detailed edition of his theological works,[37] we know more than ever, not only about his influence in alchemy, medicine and natural philosophy, but about his ethical, social, religious and political views. Paracelsus, in other words, has been rediscovered hiding in plain sight – in the world of the sixteenth century, with sixteenth-century problems to solve, with ancient and Renaissance ideas and with his Bible to guide him. He still gets idealized, and we still often get just what we're looking for. But perhaps now we are no longer looking for a hero; we have had enough of those. We know that the world is messy and that it is the messiness of the world, the confused crush of cultures and ideas, that we have to contend with. That requires something more than idealism – it requires that we be good practical reasoners, that we know how to make things, that we are at home in the world and acknowledge as relevant the insights and experiences of all kinds of people, and, most importantly, that, like Paracelsus, we never give up on moving heaven and earth for the sake of the world's well-being.

REFERENCES

Introduction

1 Herbert Kritschner et al., 'Forensisch-Anthropologische Untersuchungen der Skelettreste des Paracelsus', in *Paracelsus: Keines andern Knecht*, ed. Heinz Dopsch, Kurt Goldammer and Peter F. Kramml (Salzburg, 1993), pp. 53–61.
2 Erwin Guido Kolbenheyer, *Das Gestirn des Paracelsus* (Munich, 1921), p. 409.
3 Heinrich Schipperges, *Paracelsus Heute: Seine Bedeutung für unsere zeit* (Frankfurt am Main, 1994), p. 15.
4 Kurt Goldammer, ed., *Theophrast von Hohenheim genannt Paracelsus: Die Kärntner Schriften* (Klagenfurt, 1955), *Widmung an die Kärntner Stände* (Dedication to the Corinthian Estates), pp. 13–16.

1 Medicine Lost in a Labyrinth and the Defence of Defiant Healing

1 Elizabeth Eisenstein, *The Printing Press as an Agent of Change: Communications and Cultural Transformations in Early-modern Europe* (Cambridge, 1979), vol. 1, pp. 43ff.
2 Steven Ozment, *When Fathers Ruled: Family Life in Reformation Europe* (Cambridge, MA, 1983), pp. 126–31.
3 Steven Ozment, *Three Behaim Boys: Growing Up in Early Modern Germany* (New Haven, CT, 1990), pp. 98–103.
4 Paracelsus, *Liber de Podagricis et suis speciebus et morbis annexis*, quoted in Walter Pagel, *Paracelsus: An Introduction to Philosophical Medicine in the Era of the Renaissance* (Basel and New York, 1958), pp. 15–16.

5 Frank Hieronymus, *Theophrast und Galen: Celsus und Paracelsus* (Basel, 2005), vol. I, pt 2, pp. 378–81.
6 Karl Sudhoff, *Paracelsus: Ein deutsches Lebensbild aus der Tagen der Renaissance* (Leipzig, 1936), pp. 38–40. Hieronymus, *Theophrast und Galen*, vol. I, pt 2, p. 385.
7 Paracelsus, *Septem Defensiones: Die Verantwortung über etzlich Verunglimpfung seiner Missgönner* in *Theophrast von Hohenheim genannt Paracelsus: Die Kärntner Schriften*, ed. Kurt Goldammer et al. (Klagenfurt, 1955), p. 31.
8 Ibid., p. 35.
9 Paracelsus, *Labyrinthus Medicorum Errantium*, in *Theophrast von Hohenheim genannt Paracelsus: Die Kärntner Schriften*, pp. 69–129, p. 69.
10 Galen, *Exhortation to Study the Arts*, in *Galen: Selected Works*, trans. P. N. Singer (Oxford, 1997), p. 43.
11 Paracelsus, *Labyrinthus Medicorum Errantium*, p. 79.
12 Ibid., pp. 90–91.
13 Ibid., p. 92.
14 Ibid., pp. 93–4.
15 Ibid., p. 96.
16 Ibid., pp. 95–6.
17 Ibid., p. 98.
18 Ibid., pp. 99–100.
19 Ibid., p. 95.
20 Paracelsus, *Septem Defensiones*, p. 32.
21 Paracelsus, *Labyrinthus*, p. 73.
22 Ibid., p. 71.

2 Seeing through the Body: Nature, Disease and What the True Physician Must Know

1 Paracelsus, *Septem Defensiones: Die Verantwortung über etzlich Verunglimpfung seiner Missgönner* in *Theophrast von Hohenheim genannt Paracelsus: Die Kärntner Schriften*, ed. Kurt Goldammer et al. (Klagenfurt, 1955), p. 40.
2 Seneca, *Letters from a Stoic*, trans. Robin Campbell (London, 1969), p. 182.

3 Harry Kühnel, 'Der Arzt und seine soziale Stellung in der frühen Neuzeit', in *Paracelsus und Salzburg*, ed. Heinz Dopsch and Peter F. Kramml (Salzburg, 1994), pp. 33–44.
4 Paracelsus, *Das Buch Paragranum*, in *Paracelsus, Theophrastus Bombastus von Hohenheim, 1493–1541: Essential Theoretical Writings*, trans. Andrew Weeks (Leiden, 2008), preface, pp. 63–105.
5 Ibid., p. 129.
6 Ibid., p. 211.
7 Ibid., p. 225.
8 Ibid., p. 255.
9 Ibid., pp. 259–81.
10 Paracelsus, *Septem defensiones*, pp. 39–40.
11 *Das Buch von den tartarischen Krankheiten*, in *Die Kärntner Schriften*, pp. 146–50, 157–61. Wolfgang Schneider, *Paracelsus – Neues von seiner Tartarus-Vorlesung (1527/28)* (Braunschweig, 1985), pp. 11ff.
12 Schneider, *Tartarus-Vorlesung*, pp. 11–12.
13 Ibid., pp. 28ff.
14 Ibid., p. 13. *Das Buch von den tartarischen Krankheiten*, pp. 162–73.
15 Paracelsus, *Volumen Medicinae Paramirum*, trans. Kurt F. Leidecker (Baltimore, MD, 1949), pp. 13–23.
16 Ibid., p. 20.
17 Ibid., pp. 24–34.
18 Georges Canguilhem, *The Normal and the Pathological*, trans. Carolyn R. Fawcett and Robert S. Cohen (New York, 1989), p. 40.
19 Paracelsus, *Volumen Medicinae Paramirum*, p. 30.
20 Ibid., pp. 35–46.
21 Ibid., pp. 47–55.
22 Ibid., pp. 50–52.
23 Ibid., pp. 52–4.
24 Bettina Hitzer and Pilar León-Sanz, 'The Feeling Body and its Diseases: How Cancer went Psychosomatic in Twentieth-century Germany', *Osiris*, XXXI (2016), pp. 67–93.
25 Paracelsus, *Volumen Medicinae Paramirum*, pp. 56–63.
26 Ibid., pp. 61–2.

3 The Alchemy of Things in the Making: Medicines as Poisons and Poisons as Medicines

1 Richard Palmer, 'Pharmacy in the Republic of Venice in the Sixteenth Century', in *The Medical Renaissance of the Sixteenth Century*, ed. Andrew Wear, Roger K. French and Iain M. Lonie (Cambridge, 1985), pp. 100–117.
2 Paracelsus, *Septem Defensiones: Die Verantwortung über etzlich Verunglimpfung seiner Missgönner* in *Theophrast von Hohenheim genannt Paracelsus Die Kärntner Schriften*, ed. Kurt Goldammer, et al. (Klagenfurt, 1955), p. 60.
3 Roy Porter, *Quacks: Fakers and Charlatans in English Medicine* (Stroud, 2000), p. 39.
4 Paracelsus, *Septem Defensiones*, p. 44.
5 Ibid.
6 Ibid., p. 43.
7 Paracelsus, *Das Buch Paragranum*, in *Paracelsus, Theophrastus Bombastus von Hohenheim, 1493–1541: Essential Theoretical Writings*, trans. Andrew Weeks (Leiden, 2008), p. 221.
8 Paracelsus, 'The *Herbarius* of Paracelsus', in *Pharmacy in History*, xxxv, trans. Bruce T. Moran (1998), pp. 99–127, pp. 104–5.
9 Ibid.
10 Edgarda Künßberg, 'Die Anwendung von Heilpflanzen zur Zeit des Paracelsus und heute', in *Paracelsus und Salzburg*, ed. Heinz Dopsch and Peter F. Kramml (Salzburg, 1994), pp. 139–47.
11 Paracelsus, 'The *Herbarius* of Paracelsus', pp. 105–8.
12 Leah DeVun, *Prophecy, Alchemy, and the End of Time: John of Rupescissa in the Late Middle Ages* (New York, 2009), pp. 52ff.
13 Bruce Moran, *Distilling Knowledge: Alchemy, Chemistry, and the Scientific Revolution* (Cambridge, MA, 2005), pp. 17–25. Lawrence Principe, *The Secrets of Alchemy* (Chicago, IL, and London, 2013), pp. 62–73.
14 Otto Nowotny, 'Die chemischen Arzneimittel des Paracelsus', in *Paracelsus und Salzburg*, pp. 149–55, p. 149.
15 Frank Hieronymus, *Theophrast und Galen – Celsus und Paracelsus* (Basel, 2005), vol. I, pt 2, pp. 415–16. Joachim Telle, 'Paracelsus als Alchemiker', in *Paracelsus und Salzburg*, pp. 157–72, p. 159.
16 Paracelsus, *Das Buch Paragranum*, pp. 231–2.
17 Ibid., p. 253.

4 Pursuing the Arts Where God Has Placed Them: On the Road for the Sake of Learning

1 Frank Hieronymus, *Theophrast und Galen – Celsus und Paracelsus* (Basel, 2005), vol. 1, pt 2, pp. 415–16.
2 Paracelsus, *Septem Defensiones: Die Verantwortung über etzlich Verunglimpfung seiner Missgönner* in *Theophrast von Hohenheim genannt Paracelsus: Die Kärntner Schriften*, ed. Kurt Goldammer et al. (Klagenfurt, 1955), p. 47.
3 Ibid., p. 49.
4 Ibid., p. 50.
5 Paracelsus, *Das Buch Paragranum*, in *Paracelsus, Theophrastus Bombastus von Hohenheim, 1493–1541: Essential Theoretical Writings*, trans. Andrew Weeks (Leiden, 2008), p. 295.
6 Otto Zekert, *Doe grosse Wanderung des Paracelsus* (Ingelheim, 1965).
7 Hieronymus, *Theophrast und Galen*, vol. 1, pt 2, pp. 415–16.
8 Roland Girtler, 'Der Landfahrer Paracelsus und die Kultur des fahrenden Volkes', in *Paracelsus und Salzburg*, ed. Heinz Dopsch and Peter F. Kramml (Salzburg, 1994), pp. 393–406.
9 Roland Girtler, *Rotwelsch: Die alte Sprache der Diebe, Dirnen und Gauner* (Vienna, 1998).
10 Another, slightly later, popular text was *Die Rotwelsch Grammatic/und barlen der Wanderschaft . . .* (Basel, c. 1540).
11 Hieronymus, *Theophrast und Galen*, vol. 1, pt 2, pp. 415–16.
12 Paracelsus, *Das Buch Paragranum*, pp. 283–5.
13 Steven Ozment (compiled by), *Magdalena and Balthasar: An Intimate Portrait of Life in 16th Century Europe Revealed in the Letters of a Nuremberg Husband and Wife* (New York, 1986), pp. 124–35.
14 Frank Fürbeth, 'Zur Bedeutung des Baderwesens im Mittelalter und der frühen Neuzeit', in *Paracelsus und Salzburg*, ed. Dopsch and Kramml, pp. 463–87.
15 Frank Fürbeth, *Heilquellen in der deutschen Wissensliteratur des Spätmittelalters: zur Genese und Funktion eines Paradigmas der Wissensvermittlung am Beispiel des 'Tractatus de balneis naturalibus' von Felix Hemmerli und seiner Rezeption* (Wiesbaden, 2004).
16 Fürbeth, 'Zur Bedeutung des Baderwesens . . .', p. 468.
17 Peter F. Kramml, 'Heilbader und Bader im Leben des Paracelsus', in *Paracelsus und Salzburg*, ed. Dopsch and Kramml, pp. 525–40.

18 Ibid.
19 Jost Amman and Hans Sachs, *Das Ständebuch: 114 Holzschnitte von Jost Amman mit Reimen von Hans Sachs* (Leipzig, *c.* 1934), p. 57.
20 Thomaso Garzoni, *Piazza Universale: Das ist Allgemeiner Schauwplatz . . . aller Professionen . . .* (Frankfurt am Mayn, 1619), p. 88. Also, Robert Jütte, 'Zur Sozialgeschichte der Handwerkschirurgen im 16. Jahrhundert', in *Paracelsus und Salzburg*, ed. Dopsch and Kramml, pp. 45–60.
21 Francis R. Packard, *The Life and Times of Ambroise Paré [1510–1590], with a Translation of His Apology and the Account of His Journeys in Divers Places* (New York, 1921), p. 160.
22 Ibid., pp. 162–3.
23 Paracelsus, *Der grossenn Wundaretzney . . .* (Augsburg, 1536), *Dem hochberumpten / vil erfarnen Herren Theophrasto von Hohenhain . . .*
24 Ibid.
25 Ibid.
26 Ibid.
27 Ibid.
28 Paracelsus, *Liber de Podagricis et suis speciebus et morbis annexis*, in *Theophrast von Hoenheim . . . Sämtliche Werke*, ed. Karl Sudhoff (Munich and Berlin, 1929), vol. I, p. 342.
29 Ibid.
30 Paracelsus, *Septem Defensiones*, p. 49.
31 Ibid., p. 48.
32 Ibid., p. 47.
33 Ibid., p. 50.

5 'I Am Ashamed of Medicine': Love, Labour and the Spirit of Christ in the Transformation of the Secular World

1 Paracelsus, *Spittal Buch* (Frankfurt am Main, 1566), *Vorrede: Doctor Theophrastus / allen Artzten seinen Grüß*.
2 Paracelsus, *Septem Defensiones: Die Verantwortung* über *etzlich Verunglimpfung seiner Mißgonner*, in *Theophrast von Hohenheim genannt Paracelsus: Die Kärntner Schriften*, ed. Kurt Goldammer, et al. (Klagenfurt, 1955), p. 52.
3 Ibid., pp. 51, 54.

4 George Bernard Shaw, *The Doctor's Dilemma: A Tragedy* (Harmondsworth, 1946), pp. 10–11.

5 Paracelsus, *Das Buch Paragranum*, in *Paracelsus, Theophrastus Bombastus von Hohenheim, 1493–1541: Essential Theoretical Writings*, trans. Andrew Weeks (Leiden, 2008), p. 273.

6 Paracelsus, *Septem defensiones*, pp. 52–3.

7 Paracelsus, *Das Buch paragranum*, p. 273.

8 Paracelsus, *Septem defensiones*, pp. 53–4.

9 Ibid., p. 57.

10 Heinz Dopsch, 'Paracelsus, die Reformation und der Bauernkrieg', in *Paracelsus und Salzburg*, ed. Heinz Dopsch and Peter F. Kramml (Salzburg, 1994), pp. 201–15.

11 Ibid.

12 Steven Ozment, *Mysticism and Dissent: Religious Ideology and Social Protest in the Sixteenth Century* (New Haven, CT, 1973), pp. 1–13.

13 Paracelsus, *Auslegung über die zehen gebott gottes*, in *Sämtliche Werke 2 Abteilung: Theologische und religionsphilosophische Schriften*, ed. Kurt Goldammer (Wiesbaden, 1955), vol. VII, pp. 119–227.

14 Kurt Goldammer, *Paracelsus: Sozialethische und sozialpolitische Schriften* (Tübingen, 1952). Goldammer, 'Soziale Utopien bei Paracelsus', in *Paracelsus und Salzburg*, ed. Dopsch and Kramml, pp. 383–92.

15 Urs Leo Gantenbein, 'Paracelsus als Theologe', in *Paracelsus in Kontext der Wissenschaften seiner Zeit* (Berlin and New York, 2010), pp. 65–89.

16 Alois M. Haas, 'Paracelsus der Theologe: Die Salzburger Anfänge 1524/25', in *Paracelsus und Salzburg*, ed. Dopsch and Kramml, pp. 369–82.

17 Paracelsus, *De septem punctis idolatriae christianae*, in *Sämtliche Werke 2 Abteilung: Theologische und religionsphilosophische Schriften*, vol. III, pp. 3–4.

18 Ibid., p. 4.

19 Andrew Weeks, *Paracelsus: Speculative Theory and the Crisis of the Early Reformation* (Albany, NY, 1997).

20 Paracelsus, *De secretis secretorum theologiae*, in *Paracelsus: Sämtliche Werke 2 Abteilung*, vol. III, pp. 167–231; p. 206. Quoted in Alois M. Haas, 'Paracelsus der Theologe . . .', p. 373.

21 Paracelsus, *De septem punctis idolatriae christianae*, in *Paracelsus Sämtliche Werke 2 Abteilung*, p. 18.
22 Ibid., p. 22.
23 Ibid., p. 33.
24 Ibid., pp. 37–8.
25 Ibid., p. 54.
26 Ibid., p. 55
27 *Liber de Iustitia*, in *Sämtliche Werke 2 Abteilung* . . ., vol. II, p. 153.
28 Ibid., p. 159.
29 Ibid., pp. 157–8.
30 Ibid., *Liber de Sancta Trinitate*, vol. III, pp. 244–5.

6 Invisible Beings and Invisible Diseases: Magic and Insanity in an Age of Faith

1 Paracelsus, *Liber de nymphis, sylphis, pygmaeis et salamandris et de caeteris spiritibus*, ed. Robert Blaser, Altdeutsche Übungstexte XVI (Bern, 1960).
2 Paracelsus, *Septem Defensiones: Die Verantwortung über etzlich Verunglimpfung seiner Missgönner*, in *Theophrast von Hohenheim genannt Paracelsus: Die Kärntner Schriften*, ed. Kurt Goldammer, et al. (Klagenfurt, 1955), p. 62.
3 Paracelsus, *The Diseases that Deprive Man of his Reason*, trans. Gregory Zilboorg, in *Paracelsus: Four Treatises*, ed. Henry E. Sigerist (Baltimore, MD, and London, 1941), p. 145.
4 Ibid.
5 Ibid., p. 149.
6 Ibid., p. 152.
7 Ibid., p. 153.
8 Ibid., p. 155.
9 Ibid., pp. 177–8.
10 Ibid., p. 156.
11 Ibid., pp. 179–80.
12 Ibid., pp. 181–2.
13 Ibid., p. 181.
14 Ambroise Paré, *On Monsters and Marvels*, trans. Janis L. Pallister (Chicago, IL, 1982), pp. 38–42.

15 Paracelsus, *De causis morborum invisibilium*, in *Paracelsus, Theophrastus Bombastus von Hohenheim, 1493–1541: Essential Theoretical Writings*, trans. Andrew Weeks (Leiden, 2008), pp. 720–937, p. 803.
16 Ibid., pp. 827–39.
17 Samuel Johnson, *A History of Rasselas Prince of Abysinnia* [1759], Ch. 44, 'The Dangerous Prevalence of Imagination'.
18 Paracelsus, *De causis morborum invisibilium*, p. 763.
19 Ibid., pp. 749–53.
20 Ibid., pp. 783–9.
21 Ibid., p. 731.
22 Ibid., pp. 907, 911.
23 Ibid., p. 907.
24 Ibid., p. 935.
25 Ibid., p. 865.
26 Ibid., p. 875.
27 Andreas Tentzel, *Medicina diastatica; or, Sympatheticall Mumie . . .*, trans. Ferdinando Parkhurst (London, 1653), p. 8.

7 Inventing Paracelsus: The Use and Abuse of a Renaissance Life

1 Walter Pagel, review of Kurt Goldammer, 'Paracelsus: Socialethische und Socialpolitische Schriften', *Isis*, XLIII (1952), p. 272.
2 Franz Hartman, *Die Medizin des Threophrastus Paracelsus vom theosophischen Standpunkt betrachtet* (Leipzig, 1899); see also, *The Life of . . . Paracelsus and the Substance of his Teachings* (London, 1896).
3 Novalis, *Novalis: Auswahl und Einleitung von Walther Rehm* (Frankfurt am Main, 1956), p. 153.
4 Quoted in Kurt Goldammer, *Paracelsus in der deutschen Romantik* (*Salzburger Beiträge zu Paracelsusforschung*, vol. XX) (Vienna, 1980), p. 25.
5 Novalis, *Novalis: Auswahl*, p. 202.
6 Ibid., p. 204.
7 Ibid.
8 Ibid., p. 61.
9 Ibid., p. 198.
10 Ibid.

11 Goldammer, *Paracelsus in der deutschen Romantik*, pp. 23–46.

12 Ingonda Hannesschläger, 'Echte und vermeintliche Porträts des Paracelsus', in *Paracelsus und Salzburg*, ed. Heinz Dopsch and Peter F. Kramml (Salzburg, 1994), pp. 217–49.

13 Friedrich Schelling, *Ideen zu einer Philosophie der Natur* [1797], in *Friedrich Wilhelm Joseph von Schellings sämmtliche Werke*, vol II (Stuttgart and Augsburg, 1857), pp. 217–18.

14 David Boswell Reid, 'History and Present State of Chemical Science', *Edinburgh Review, or Critical Journal for October 1829 . . . January 1830* (Edinburgh, 1830), pp. 256–76; pp. 258–9.

15 John Haydn Baker, *Browning and Wordsworth* (Madison, WI, 2004), pp. 36–72. Shou-ren Wang, *The Theatre of the Mind: a Study of Unacted Drama in Nineteenth-century England* (New York, 1990), pp. 58–69. Marion Little, *Essays on Robert Browning* (London, 1899), pp. 41–118.

16 Robert Browning, *Paracelsus* [1835], in *The Works of Robert Browning*, vol. I (New York, 1966; repr. 1912), pp. 39–168.

17 Ibid., p. 55, lines 533–5.

18 Ibid., p. 62, lines 785–7.

19 Ibid., p. 62, lines 775–7; p. 55, line 527.

20 Ibid., p. 116, lines 991–6.

21 Ibid., p. 53, lines 474–6.

22 Ibid., pp. 161–8, lines 636–885.

23 Ibid., p. 168, lines 885–8.

24 Ibid., p. 168, lines 894–903.

25 Udo Benzenhöfer, '"War's Ernset, War's Spiel?": Bemerkungen zu Arthur Schnitzlers "Paracelsus" Einakter', in *Paracelsus und Salzburg*, ed. Dopsch and Kramml, pp. 121–7.

26 Quoted in Herbert I. Kupper and Hilda S. Rollman-Branch, 'Freud and Schnitzler – (Doppelgänger)', *Journal of the American Psychoanalytical Association*, VII (1959), pp. 109–10.

27 Arthur Schnitzler, *Gesammelte Werke von Authir Schnitzler in zwei Abteilung* (Berlin, 1918), vol. II, *Abteilung* 2, pp. 9–57.

28 Ibid., pp. 40–41.

29 Ibid., p. 57.

30 Ibid., p. 49.

31 Ibid., p. 57.

32 Martha Sills-Fuchs, *Paracelsus und Wir: Eine Studie über die Persönlichkeit des Theophrastus von Hohenheim* (Planegg, 1941), pp. 37ff.

33 Udo Benzenhöfer, '"Propaganda das Herzen": Zum "Paracelsus"-Film von Georg W. Pabst', in *Medizin im Spielfilm des Nationalsozialismus*, ed. Udo Benzenhöfer and Wolfgang U. Eckart (Tecklenburg, 1990), pp. 52–68. Lee Atwell, *G.W. Pabst* (Boston, MA, 1977).

34 Peter F. Kramml, 'Zwischen Rezeption, Kult, Vermarkung und Vereinnahmung: Die Paracelsus-Tradition in der Stadt Salzburg', in *Paracelsus und Salzburg*, ed. Dopsch and Kramml, pp. 279–346. Kramml, 'Verwirkliche und nicht realisierte Salzburger Paracelsus-Projekte in der Zeit des Dritten Reiches', in *Paracelsus und das Reich: 55. Paracelsustag 2006* (*Salzburger Beiträge zur Paracelsusforschung*, vol. XL) (Salzburg, 2007), pp. 57–90.

35 Quoted in Kramml, 'Zwishen Rezeption', p. 315.

36 Ibid.

37 Urs Leo Gantenbein, ed., *Neue Paracelsus-Edition* (Berlin, 2008–).

SELECT BIBLIOGRAPHY

Standard German Sources for the Works of Paracelsus

Paracelsus, *Die Kärntner Schriften*, ed. Kurt Goldammer et al. (Klagenfurt, 1956)

—, *Sämtliche Werke*, ed. Karl Sudhoff and Wilhelm Matthiessen (Munich and Berlin, 1922–33)

—, *Sämtliche Werke: Nach der 10bändigen Huserschen Gesamtausgabe, 1589–1591, zum erstenmals in neuzeitliches Deutsch übersetzt* . . ., ed. Bernard Aschner (Jena, 1926–32)

—, *Sämtliche Werke: Zweite Abteilung: Theologische und religionsphilosophische Schriften*, ed. Kurt Goldammer (Wiesbaden, 1955–)

—, *Vita beata: vom glückseligen Leben (Neue Paracelsus-Edition, Theologische Werke*, vol. I), ed. Urs Leo Gantenbein in collaboration with Michael Baumann and Detlef Roth (Berlin, 2008)

For English Readers

Paracelsus, *Four Treatises of Theophrastus von Hohenheim, Called Paracelsus*, ed. Henry E. Sigerist (Baltimore, MD, 1941)

—, *Paracelsus (Theophrastus von Hohenheim), 1493–1541: Essential Theoretical Writings*, ed. and trans. Andrew Weeks (Leiden and Boston, MA, 2008)

—, *Volumen Medicinae Paramirum of Theophrastus von Hohenheim, Called Paracelsus*, trans. Kurt F. Leidecker (Baltimore, MD, 1949)

For General Discussions in Both German and English

Ball, Philip, *The Devil's Doctor: Paracelsus and the World of Renaissance Magic and Science* (New York, 2006)

Benzenhöfer, Udo, *Paracelsus* (Reinbek, 1997)

Cislo, Amy Eisen, *Paracelsus's Theory of Embodiment: Conception and Gestation in Early Modern Europe* (London, 2010)

Classen, Albrecht., ed., *Paracelsus im Kontext der Wissenschaften seiner Zeit* (Berlin and New York, 2010)

Crone, Hugh, *Paracelsus: The Man who Defied Medicine: His Real Contribution to Medicine and Science* (Melbourne, 2004)

Dopsch, Heinz, Kurt Goldammer and Peter F. Kramml, eds, *Paracelsus (1493–1541): 'Keines andern Knecht'* (Salzburg, 1993)

Frietsch, Ute, *Häresie und Wissenschaft: eine Genealogie der Paracelsischen Alchemie* (Munich, 2013)

Goldammer, Kurt, *Paracelsus: Sozialethische und sozialpolitische Schriften* (Tübingen, 1952)

—, *Paracelsus: Natur und Offenbarung* (Hannover-Rirchrode, 1953)

Grell, Ole Peter, ed., *Paracelsus: The Man and his Reputation, his Ideas and their Transformation* (Leiden and Boston, MA, 1998)

Hemleben, Johannes, *Paracelsus: Revolutionär, Arzt und Christ* (Stuttgart, 1973)

Kaiser, Ernst, *Paracelsus* (Reinbek bei Hamburg, 1969)

Jütte, Robert, ed., *Paracelsus heute: im Lichte der Natur* (Heidelberg, 1994)

Pagel, Walter, *Paracelsus: An Introduction to Philosophical Medicine in the Era of the Renaissance* (Basel and New York, 1958)

Schwedt, Georg, *Paracelsus in Europa: auf den Spuren des Arztes und Naturforschers* (Munich, 1993)

Sudhoff, Karl, *Paracelsus: Ein deutsches Lebensbild aus den Tagen der Renaissance* (Leipzig, 1936)

Webster, Charles, *Paracelsus: Medicine, Magic and Mission at the End of Time* (New Haven, CT, and London, 2008)

Weeks, Andrew, *Paracelsus: Speculative Theory and the Crisis of the Early Reformation* (Albany, NY, 1997)

ACKNOWLEDGEMENTS

The invitation to write this book came at just the right moment. I had decided, after forty years of teaching, to enter 'phased-in' retirement. That decision provided a crucial element of all writing, namely the temporal space in which to do it. I had been an interested observer of Paracelsus studies for just as many years, having first gained the acquaintance of well-known Paracelsus scholars while a visitor at research centres in the German cities of Kassel and Marburg during the early 1980s. The texts of Paracelsus and the debates and research surrounding his life and work became a consistent focus thereafter, and although my own scholarly inquiries took a different tack over the years, the change in professional obligations now made it possible to return to a lingering passion. Writing about Paracelsus takes courage, and I admire those who have spent lifetimes in Paracelsian studies. A little book like this one, with its narrow limitations of bibliography and reference, does not allow me to acknowledge all those whose writings have been influential. Singling out some would be to slight others. I have learned from them all. What is important to acknowledge more specifically, however, are the spaces in which reading and writing took place. In that regard, I do wish to refer to the hospitality offered to me by the Wellcome Library, London, and by the Max Planck Institute for the History of Science, Berlin. In addition, because starting a new dimension in life involved moving to a new place, I wish to recognize friends and neighbours in Ellison Park, Waltham, Massachusetts, especially Wayne and Roberta McCarthy, who offered much needed community and a site of conversation and enjoyment during the time this book came into being.

PHOTO ACKNOWLEDGEMENTS

The author and publishers wish to express their thanks to the below sources of illustrative material and/or permission to reproduce it:

From *Andreae Alciati . . . Emblematum liber* (Augsburg, 1531), photo Wellcome Collection: 6; from Jean-Jacques Boissard, *Icones et Effigies* (Frankfurt, 1645), photo Wellcome Collection: 20; from Robert Browning, *Paracelsus* (London, 1899): 22; from Hieronymus Brunschwig, *Liber de arte distillandi* (Strasbourg, 1512), photos Wellcome Collection: 9, 10; photo Everett Collection Historical / Alamy Stock Photo: 1; from Hans von Gersdorf, *Feldtbuch der Wundartzney, newlich getruckt und gebessert* (Strasburg, 1530), photo Wellcome Collection: 15; from Conrad Gesner, *Corpus Venetum de Balneis* (Venice, 1553), photo Wellcome Collection: 11; from Joannes de Ketham, *Fasciculus medicine . . .* (Venice, 1495), photo Wellcome Collection: 3; Kunstmuseum Basel, reproduced by kind permission (Open Access): 12; from *Musæum Hermeticum Reformatum et Amplificatum* (Frankfurt, 1678), photo Wellcome Collection: 19; Musée du Louvre, Paris: 21; from *Nova Reperta*, an undated collection of engravings after Jan van der Straet (Stradanus), photo Wellcome Collection: 7; from Theophrastus Paracelsus von Hohenheim, *Der ander Theyl der grossen Wundartzeney* (Frankfurt, 1536), photo Wellcome Collection: 16; from Auroleus Theophrastus Paracelsus, *Opus chyrurgicum* (Frankfurt, 1565), photo Wellcome Collection: 14; from *Philosophiae Magnae, des Edlen, Hochgelährten, Vielerfarlen vnd weitberhümeten Herrn, D. Avreoli Theophrasti von Hohenhaim, Paracelsi genandt . . .* (Cöln, 1567): 1; from *Rechter Gebrauch der Alchimei* (Frankfurt, 1531), photo ETH-Bibliothek Zürich: 8; from Hans Sachs, *Eygentliche Beschreibung aller Stände auff Erden hoher und nidriger, geistlicher und weltlicher, aller Künsten, Handwerken und Händeln* (Frankfurt, 1568), photo Wellcome Collection: 13; from Hartmann Schedel, *Liber chronicarum*

(Nuremberg, 1493), photo Special Collections, University of Nevada, Reno: 5, 17; from Andreas Vesalius, *De humani corporis fabrica* (Basel, 1543), photo Wellcome Collection: 4; The Wellcome Collection (photo Wellcome Collection): 18; Wellcome Institute, London (photo Wellcome Collection): 23; photo Wellcome Collection: 2.

INDEX

Illustration numbers are in *italics*